PRAISE FOR
FROM DREAM TO DESTINY

Robert Morris has shined the light on the human dilemma—
diversions from the main road. His book *From Dream to Destiny* is a
cutting-edge road map that offers hope without hype. Even more
significantly, Pastor Morris humbly reveals life-changing power points,
as he himself has wrestled with destiny killers. *From Dream to Destiny*
crackles with high energy. It is a rocketing read.

MICHAEL D. EVANS
Author, *New York Times* Best-Seller *The American Prophecies* and
Beyond Iraq: The Next Move

Robert Morris is a new and rising voice in today's Church world—
a man of God purely motivated, wisely and biblically balanced, and
prompted by a shepherd's heart for the sheep of Christ's pasture.
His words will feed, nourish and lift your soul.

JACK W. HAYFORD
Author, *Living the Spirit-Formed Life*
Founding Pastor, The Church On The Way
Van Nuys, California

From Dream to Destiny pulls out valuable lessons learned from
the biblical account of the life of Joseph. Robert has provided possible
answers to the why questions we all face—Why am I going through this
trial? Why doesn't God hear my prayer? You will find this book
to be applicable to all age groups.

CHAD HENNINGS
Three-Time Super Bowl Champion, Dallas Cowboys
Former Air Force Fighter Pilot

This is required reading for all believers! At a time when
I most needed a fresh revelation from the Lord, I was introduced to
the messages in *From Dream to Destiny*. I have since taken thousands of
others through this teaching. I urge you to study this material
that will hasten your journey toward your destiny.

JAMES T. MEEKS

Pastor, Salem Baptist Church
Chicago, Illinois

My pastor, Robert Morris, uses Joseph's life story to illustrate 10 tests
that will surely come our way. How we learn from each test and
respond will determine whether we step into the fullness of what God
has planned for us. Robert inspires us to remain faithful and focused
on Jesus, whose destiny for us is bigger than we can determine.

JAMES ROBISON

President, LIFE Outreach International

FROM DREAM TO DESTINY

ROBERT MORRIS

BETHANYHOUSE

a division of Baker Publishing Group
Minneapolis, Minnesota

Published by Bethany House Publishers
11400 Hampshire Avenue South
Bloomington, Minnesota 55438
www.bethanyhouse.com

Bethany House Publishers is a division of
Baker Publishing Group, Grand Rapids, Michigan

Bethany House edition published 2014
ISBN 978-0-7642-1710-4

Previously published by Regal Books

Printed in the United States of America

The Library of Congress has cataloged the original edition as follows:
Morris, Robert (Robert Preston), 1961–
    From dream to destiny / Robert Morris.
       p. cm.
    Includes bibliographical references.
    ISBN 978-0-8307-3675-1
      1. Christian life—Biblical teaching. 2. Success—Biblical teaching. 3. Joseph (Son of Jacob)
    I. Title.
    BS680.C47M667 2005
    248.4–dc22   2004027348

17 18 19 20   7 6 5 4 3 2

CONTENTS

FULFILLING YOUR DESTINY

It caught me completely by surprise.

As I was preparing to speak to a large group of 18- to 29-year-olds at an area church, I found myself praying fervently for direction about my message. I carried a sense of obligation and a strong desire to bring these young adults something from the heart of God Himself. Perhaps it was because I knew how many critical, life-changing decisions are made in those early years. Maybe it was because I had been a foolish, self-destructive young man of 19 when the Lord finally captured me with His love and completely transformed my life.

Whatever the reason, I desperately wanted to know what God desired to say to that group. That's when the surprise came.

In a moment, the Spirit of God began to flood my mind with an outline for a series of messages about a young man named Joseph—and the vital lessons he learned on the way to fulfilling his destiny. The message themes came faster than I could write them down, yet they remained burned into my heart and memory as the beginning of a powerful "prophetic word." This word concerned the destiny God has planned for the current generation—for those of us who desire to be used in these remarkable days in which we live.

In that startling encounter with God's Spirit, I began to see with fresh depth how Joseph had been destined for great power, destined to be an instrument of God's deliverance for humanity and yet had to endure great testing along the way. How at the tender age of 17 he had received a glimpse of that destiny in a dream—but failed to understand the journey toward his destiny had only just begun.

If you're familiar with the biblical account in Genesis, you know that it wasn't until Joseph was 30 years old that he stepped into the first phase of the extraordinary destiny God had ordained for his life. In fact, it was only through hard lessons learned in those years of testing that God was able to equip Joseph—and only through those same lessons that Joseph was found faithful to walk out that destiny and to fulfill the dream to the fullest.

Every one of us has a dream, and every one of us has a destiny. The question is, How do we travel from the dream to the destiny—and what happens on the way?

Perhaps you have some dreams that are yet to be fulfilled, a destiny that you may have caught a glimpse of. You may have even compared yourself with others who seem to be walking in their destiny, and perhaps you have wondered what is hindering you from stepping into yours.

I believe that the book you now hold in your hands—the fruit of the study that began with a prophetic word—will bring you exciting answers to many of those questions. From the life of Joseph, you will learn vital truths about the tests that wait for you on the road to destiny—tests that you must pass if you are to step into the fullness of what God has planned for you.

We all have dreams for our families, dreams for our finances, dreams for our chosen vocations—but right now I want to challenge you to dream a little bigger. Allow God to stir in your heart *His* dream for you. I promise, His dream for you is better. His destiny for you is bigger.

You see, God's thoughts for you are higher than your thoughts. His plans for you are better than your plans. He has a dream for you, and it is better than your dream. He has a destiny in mind for you, and it is not only bigger than you currently imagine, it also is bigger than you *can ever* imagine. You can't dream a bigger dream than God can dream!

Certainly, each person's dream is unique; but somehow each one is supernaturally intertwined with the master dream of our loving heavenly Father: to reconcile His lost children to Himself. Toward the fulfillment of His dream, God has assigned a role for each one of us—a destiny that is essential to His plans. No two roles are exactly alike, but they are all equally important to God. Thus, there are things He has created you to do that only you can accomplish. The same is true for me.

You may not pastor a church or preach on a regular basis like I do, but that does not mean your assignment is any less important than mine. Each one of us has a unique assignment from God. And if you don't do it, it won't get done!

That is why I believe these messages about Joseph are so vital in this hour. I believe a day is coming (and has already begun) when we will see an outpouring of the latter rain and, as a result, a worldwide harvest of souls. Each of us has a part to play—and our parts will be fulfilled only to the extent that our God-given destinies have been fulfilled.

To put it bluntly, we are not supposed to be sitting around, waiting for the Rapture while people around us are heading toward hell.

I believe God ignited the fire of this message in my heart that day because we carry a special calling to bring in the end-time harvest. Like Joseph, we are destined for great power and great influence. And like Joseph, we will have to pass great tests if we are to step into that influence and bring God's provision of salvation to this world.

This message is for all of us: It is for me and for you, wherever you are, whatever your age. Every one of us is on a journey toward a destiny, and every one of us is destined to do great things for God and His kingdom.

Joseph encountered 10 tests on his way from the dream to the destiny—tests that he ultimately passed, tests that enabled him to inherit the promise. They are relevant because these are tests each of us will face as we press toward the dream God has given us. Like Joseph, we will find our destiny waiting on the other side. Like Joseph, we must pass these tests to get there.

Would you like to find out how? Read on.

THE
PRIDE TEST

It was Sunday morning, and things were beginning to quiet down at the prayer center for James Robison's ministry. Phone volunteers were finishing their 5 A.M. shifts and heading off to church. The only two people left to man the phones were myself and Terry Redman—a good friend, who also happens to be the son-in-law of James Robison.

It was an interesting series of events that had led me to the prayer center that day. Although still in my early 20s, I had already been involved in public ministry for several years. Things had happened pretty fast after I surrendered my life to Jesus Christ at the age of 19. Only 10 months after being saved, I met James Robison, and he asked me to start traveling with him, speaking to junior and senior high school assemblies. So I had not even been a Christian for a year when I began to travel and preach the gospel. Pretty heady stuff for someone so young (and even younger in the Lord!).

Though I started out speaking at public schools, it wasn't long before I was preaching at crusades. Eventually, James was even gracious enough to give me a title: associate evangelist. Wow—I was only 20 years old, but because of my association with James, I was already involved in television, preaching to large crowds, and even had a title to prove that I was a bona-fide evangelist!

It seemed to me that the favor of God was on everything I touched. What a destiny lay before me! What could stop me now?

In retrospect, it's clear that an enemy called pride had begun to creep into my life. Slowly, stealthily, thoughts of pride began to take up residence in my mind—thoughts that could not coexist with a proper reverence for a holy God.

By the time I was 25, I had become far too accustomed to hearing people tell me how gifted I was. I began to listen to this praise. Worse, I was beginning to *expect* it. People would say to me, "You are so gifted—you can do anything!" And with all the wisdom of my 25 years, I began to believe them. I started thinking, *Man, I'm something. I'm successful!*

Deep down, I knew I was prideful, but I didn't know what to do about it. The more that pride grew, the more it seemed to stand in my way. So I began to pray about it, asking God for help. I said, "God, I know I have pride. I know my insecurity makes me vulnerable to it. I need to be free of this, but I don't know what to do!"

One day as I was praying along these lines, I asked the Lord, "What can I do about this? Is there anything I can do to deal with the pride in my life?"

His answer didn't exactly thrill me. I sensed Him telling me, "Well, here's a thought. You could step out of the ministry and just take a regular job."

I suppose my response didn't exactly thrill Him either. I said, "Yes, that is a thought, Lord. It's a *bad* thought, but it *is* a thought."

Seriously though, the religious part of me couldn't imagine that it would be God's will for me to leave the ministry. (After all, I was being used so mightily by Him!) But try as I might, I could not get rid of that thought. It got stronger and stronger until the Lord orchestrated the circumstances for me to step out of ministry. I finally did what the Lord suggested: I stepped out of the ministry and started looking for a job.

But I couldn't find one!

I quickly discovered that I wasn't as valuable as I had presumed. Think about it. When you've been an evangelist, what do you list as your skills on a job application? Strong preaching ability? Gives excellent altar calls? Exegetes well? From a practical standpoint, you simply don't have a lot of qualifications for a regular job.

After much searching, I finally found a job—as a security guard at a Motel 6. That was the only job I could get. Now you must remember, people had told me that I was so gifted that I could do anything. But it didn't take long for me to learn that wasn't true. I learned that without God's blessing, you can't do anything. It is only the blessing of God that causes us to have true success. And so it was that I learned a very important lesson—a lesson I would never have learned without first stepping out of ministry.

After a month of working nights as a security guard at Motel 6, I felt I had made great strides toward humility. I decided that perhaps I was ready to return to ministry. So I checked back with James Robison's ministry to see if they had any job openings. I was happy to discover that they needed a morning supervisor at their prayer center, from 5 A.M. to 2 P.M. That sure sounded better than the "graveyard shift" I had been working at the Motel 6. So I took the job.

Keep in mind, I previously had been an associate evangelist there. Now I was back at the ministry, but working as a prayer partner—and God was continuing to do His pride-killing work in my heart.

As I said, on that particular morning only Terry and I were left in the room, and I was busy on the phone, talking with a woman who had called for prayer. Before we got off the phone, she said to me, "You sound so familiar." So I began to fill her in on exactly who I was. "Oh, you probably recognize me from one of the crusades," I said. "I'm an associate evangelist here at the ministry, and I used to travel and preach crusades."

The room seemed strangely quiet as I hung up the phone. My good friend Terry turned to me and I noticed that he had taken his phone off the hook.

"Can I talk to you a minute?" he asked.

"Robert," he said gently, "I am so happy about what you are doing right now. I realize most people would not be willing to do what you are doing, and I'm so glad to see that you are allowing God to work in this area of your life. But I want to ask you something. Why did you tell that woman that you were an associate evangelist? You're not anymore, and you know that. You know what you are—you're a prayer partner."

Feeling defensive, I said, "Well, I *used* to be an associate evangelist, and I just thought it would bless her to know that." Bless *her!* My words seemed hollow and contrived, even to me.

I really wasn't quite sure why I had told her that, so I asked Terry a question. "When you're on the phone with someone, don't you ever tell them that you're James Robison's son-in-law?"

"No."

"Don't you think it would bless someone who calls in, to know that they got to pray with James's son-in-law?"

Terry drew a deep breath. "Well," he replied, "if they are blessed by *that*, then they are being blessed for the wrong reason."

I will never forget the words that followed.

"Robert, I love you, man. But you are going to have to get to the place where you have your identity in Christ, and not in what you do or in who you are."

The words that Terry spoke that day pierced my heart. Yet God took those words and began to use them in my life. In fact, He continues to use them to this day.

You see, although I didn't know it at the time, I was in the very early stages of a journey toward my destiny in God. God had given me a glimpse of how He wanted to use me and of the destiny He had in mind for me. But now I was in the middle of an important test—and I would have to pass that test before I could move into the next phase along the path to destiny.

I'm so glad God doesn't "flunk" any of us on our tests. If He did, He surely could have written F on the pages of my life many times! No, each time we fail, He graciously writes "Redo"—and allows us to keep retaking the test until we pass it. Why? Because it is only when we pass the test that we will be able to step into the destiny He has planned for us.

At that point I had yet to learn that great destiny carries with it great responsibilities—responsibilities that require strong character. It's easy to get excited about God's plans, without having any idea about the strengths we will need in order to fulfill them. But He knows. He knows everything about us. He knows the dreams He has for us and what it will take to get the job done. And He wants us to be fully equipped.

Seasons of Testing

We may love God—and we may even have big dreams in our hearts that He Himself has placed there. All of that is wonderful. But without the character of God on the inside of us, we won't get very far. First Corinthians 10:13 says God will never allow us "to be tempted beyond what [we] are able." (In other words, He won't allow us to get into a situation that we don't have the strength to handle!) That's why He allows us to go through tests on the way from the dream to the destiny—tests that prepare us to succeed when we get there.

I wasn't the first young man to find myself seemingly sidetracked from a God-given dream. Thousands of years ago, a young man named Joseph also received a dream from God. And it wasn't long before he also found himself in the middle of an unexpected test—a test that probably didn't seem to line up at all with the dream God had given him.

That test was only the beginning of a long season of testing for Joseph. In fact, he went on to experience 10 distinct tests on the way to his destiny. But after passing those tests, he stepped into the glorious fulfillment of God's dream. Walking out the fullness of that dream was not only a great blessing to Joseph, but also to hundreds of thousands of others who came after him.

I believe every one of us will encounter these same 10 tests on the way from our dreams to our destinies. And like Joseph, we will have to pass these tests in order to see the dream fulfilled.

The Pride Test: Revealing the Pride Within

Interestingly enough, Joseph's first test was the same one I found myself facing as a young man that day at the prayer center. It's what I call the Pride Test and it is a very important one. Joseph experienced it. I experienced it. And I'm convinced every one of us will have to pass this test before we can move from our dreams to our destinies.

Genesis 37 describes how Joseph first received his dream from God—and how he handled it when the dream came.

Joseph, being seventeen years old, was feeding the flock with his brothers. And the lad was with the sons of Bilhah and the sons of Zilpah, his father's wives; and Joseph brought a bad report of them to his father. Now Israel loved Joseph more than all his children, because he was the son of his old age. Also he made him a tunic of many colors. But when his brothers saw that their father loved him more than all his brothers, they hated him and could not speak peaceably to him. Now Joseph had a dream, and he told it to his brothers; and they hated him even more. So he said to them, "Please hear this dream which I have dreamed: There we were, binding sheaves in the field. Then behold, my sheaf arose and also stood upright; and indeed your sheaves stood all around and bowed down to my sheaf." And his brothers said to him, "Shall you indeed reign over us? Or shall you indeed have dominion over us?" So they hated him even more for his dreams and for his words. Then he dreamed still another dream and told it to his brothers, and said, "Look, I have dreamed another dream. And this time, the sun, the moon, and the eleven stars bowed down to me." So he told it to his father and his brothers; and his father rebuked him and said to him, "What is this dream that you have dreamed? Shall your mother and I and your brothers indeed come to bow down to the earth before you?" And his brothers envied him, but his father kept the matter in mind (Gen. 37:2-11).

First of all, we have to marvel at the fact that Joseph shared his dream so enthusiastically with older, bigger brothers—especially when the Bible tells us that his brothers already "hated him and could not speak peaceably to him" (Gen. 37:4). I guess it's no surprise that their response was less than enthusiastic. Still, Joseph was pretty excited about the dream that God had given him. Regardless of the consequences, he just had to let everyone know about it!

Little did he know what lay between him and his dream: Although Joseph was 17 years old when he received his dreams from God, it wasn't until he was 30 years old that he began to fulfill it (see Gen. 41:46). So we can see that 13 long years went by before Joseph began to walk in the first steps of his destiny. What could explain the long time lag between the dream and its fulfillment?

After all, it seemed obvious from the dream that Joseph was destined for great power and influence. Indeed, his brothers were envious after hearing the dream—although they had mocked the dream to his face. Joseph's father didn't discount the dream entirely either. The Bible says that his father rebuked him about it, but then he "kept the matter in mind" (Gen. 37:11).

But there was a test on the horizon for Joseph. Something was standing in the way of Joseph's moving toward that destiny God had shown him. And Joseph was about to have an opportunity to face that obstacle and deal with it. The reason for that test was really quite simple: Joseph had pride in his heart.

It is important to notice that Joseph had pride in his heart *before* he ever got the dream from God. The Bible says that Joseph was keeping the flock with his brothers, and he "brought a bad report of them to his father" (Gen. 37:2). Never mind what the bad report was about. Perhaps Joseph's brothers weren't exactly perfect, and they may indeed have deserved some correction. But this verse reveals that Joseph thought of *himself* as someone qualified to make that type of judgment about them. He even took it upon himself to see that they were corrected, although they were older and more experienced. Any time we pass judgment on the behavior of others, it reveals a prideful attitude on our part. And it seems that Joseph had a prideful attitude.

God knew that Joseph was prideful—yet God still gave him the dream. Certainly Joseph's destiny is evidence of the biblical principle which assures us "The gifts and callings of God are without repentance." God had a big destiny in mind for Joseph—and He knew that prideful attitude would have to go, if Joseph were to succeed.

You may wonder why God would give such a huge dream to such a young man—especially when He knew that Joseph already had pride in his heart. Why not wait until he was a little older, a little wiser, a little more humble, perhaps? The answer is really quite simple. God planned for Joseph to step into the dream at the age of 30—and He knew that could never happen until Joseph had dealt with that pride. So God allowed Joseph to see the big dream at 17, so the pride in his heart could be exposed and dealt with.

Joseph failed the first test, yes—but God knew that he would fail it. Remember, although we may fail, we never actually flunk a test with God—we just keep taking it over and over again until we pass it. In giving Joseph the dream, God was helping him to take the first necessary steps toward his destiny. How? By revealing the pride in Joseph's heart and by allowing Joseph to start working on passing that test.

Every one of us deals with pride, and every one of us must pass the Pride Test some day. We may have to go lower and lower before we finally pass it—but God will see to it that we pass this test somehow. Never forget the truth of the promise found in Philippians 1:6: "Being confident of this very thing, that He who has begun a good work in you will complete it until the day of Jesus Christ."

God has big dreams for all of us—and He will persevere as He seeks to get rid of anything that stands in the way.

God has big dreams for all of us, just as He did for Joseph—and He will persevere as He seeks to get rid of anything that stands in the way.

God may have given you a big dream and revealed a big destiny He has planned for you. But if you become prideful about it, you won't be able to step into that destiny. Remember, if you can't handle the dream, you will never be able to handle the destiny. And God will not allow you to be tempted beyond your strength.

So if you seem to be stuck between your dream and your destiny, allow God to work in your heart. He may have given you a big dream now in order to reveal an issue that was already there—so that you can deal with it and move on. He wants to get you to the place where He can lead you into your destiny.

Dealing with Pride

It shouldn't surprise us that pride is often the first and most frequent test we face. After all, pride is the ultimate "original sin." It is the sin that caused Lucifer to fall (Isaiah 14:12-13). And it was an appeal to pride that Satan used to tempt Adam and Eve to fall as well (see Gen. 3:5). Obviously, pride and falling are closely linked (see Prov. 16:18).

If we're honest, we will all admit to having dealt with pride at some time or another. Even if we've passed the Pride Test several times already, we will probably continue to take this test as long as we live, just at different levels. It's a little bit like a foundational subject in school, such as math. We may pass it at the third-grade level, but then we need to pass it at the fourth-grade level. Once we have passed it at the fourth-grade level, we need to pass at the fifth-grade level, and so on.

The good news is that each time we pass a test with God, we will receive a new level of responsibility in His kingdom. But with each new level of responsibility, we will face a new level of testing in the area of pride.

The Problem Is Your Tongue

Here's a simple guideline for everyone who wants to pass the Pride Test: When you get the dream—don't brag about it! Joseph made that mistake when he told his brothers his dreams. The Scriptures say that his brothers hated him "for his dreams *and for his words*" (Gen. 37:8, emphasis added). It wasn't just Joseph's dreams that offended his brothers—it was the way he talked about his dreams, the way he talked about himself. In other words, Joseph was bragging.

Now, bragging is a sign of immaturity, but we have to give Joseph a little bit of a break here. After all, he was only 17. But 17-year-olds aren't the only ones who brag. Unfortunately, many 35-year-olds, 50-year-olds and 60-year-olds brag as well. It seems that every person is susceptible to boasting and self-promotion, just as every person is susceptible to pride and insecurity.

If we want to move toward our destinies, we're going to have to learn to control our tongues. Why? Because in the Bible James tells us that whoever can control his or her tongue is a perfect person (see Jas. 3:2)—able to control the rest of his or her body as well. So if you want to deal with the pride in your life, you're going to have to control your tongue. If you can't control your words, you'll never reach God's destiny for you.

This doesn't apply to words of vanity only. It also applies to words of anger, criticism or any other words that are contrary to God's words and ways. But the area of bragging is certainly a good place to start! So don't brag about the call of God on your life. Don't brag about the gifts you have. Don't brag about the things you've done for God or the things you're going to do for Him.

I've noticed that as soon as we start talking about all that God has done through us, it seems that He immediately stops doing things through us. God will not share His glory with another. So when we begin to take the glory that is meant for God and bask in it ourselves, the anointing of the Holy Spirit leaves us. Let's keep the conversation on God and all that He has done, not on us. When the focus is on us, or even on what God has done through us, we are taking a stroll down the slippery slope of pride.

Unfortunately, in order for some of us to get a handle on our bragging, we simply need to stop talking for a while—because when we talk, we brag! When we talk, we talk about ourselves. If that sounds rather harsh, let me say that I speak from experience. I feel like an expert, because I've failed at this subject so many times!

Years ago, I asked my wife, Debbie, to help me in this area. I was beginning to wonder if perhaps I had a tendency to talk too much—especially about myself. So I begged her to be honest with me about it. At first she was reluctant to give me an answer. But after a lot of coaxing, she confirmed my suspicions—and then some.

In her kind and loving way, she let me know I was on the right track. So I enlisted her help in changing my behavior pattern. I said to her, "When we're out to eat with people, will you nudge me if I'm talking too much? If I start talking about myself, give me a little kick under the table."

My legs were black and blue for months! (Sadly, I usually didn't respond to the first two or three kicks!) But I really did want help so that I could grow in this area. I needed to control my tongue, and I'm so grateful Debbie was willing to help me.

If you have a problem with what is coming out of your mouth, you need to take a good look inside your heart.

The Real Problem Is in Your Heart

It is a good thing to get control of the tongue, but there is another important element we need to understand. If we have a problem with bragging, it is not a mouth problem only. The problem may seem to be mouth centered, but it really begins in the heart.

This is precisely the point Jesus made in Matthew 12:34 when He said, "For out of the abundance of the heart the mouth speaks." And in Matthew 15:18 He says, "But those things which proceed out of the mouth come from the heart, and they defile a man."

The Bible makes it clear that if you have a problem with what is coming out of your mouth, you need to take a good look inside your heart—

because whatever is in your heart will eventually come out of your mouth.

Have you ever noticed that pride always has to be heard? Pride has to give its opinion every time, whether or not an opinion has been asked for. Pride has to have a voice. Pride has to tell everybody who he is, what he's done and all the things he is going to do for God. Pride can never just be quiet.

It is good to bridle the tongue, and we all need discipline in that area. But if pride is in your heart, it will eventually find its way out of your mouth, no matter how much self-discipline you apply (or how many kicks under the table you receive).

What really needs to happen is for God to do a work in your heart. Because when God gets inside your heart, He can start to deal with the roots of pride.

The Root of Pride

One reason pride has a tendency to keep cropping up is that we often try to deal with the "fruit" of it rather than getting to the "root" of it. When we see the fruit of pride in our lives, we like to get out our pruning shears and snip away at the leaves—perhaps even lop off a few branches here and there. But if we don't deal with the root of pride, it will just keep sprouting up in our lives, prolonging our testing and delaying our destiny.

There is a root of pride that must be removed, or we will continue to struggle in this area. That root is insecurity.

If you know a prideful person, you know a person who is actually insecure. He or she may be trying to mask that insecurity with big, pompous-sounding words (which certainly look and sound like pride)—but it is actually insecurity.

To put it another way, the fruit, pride, is what the world sees—because of what comes out of our mouths. But what they don't see is the insecurity in our hearts—this insecurity is the cause of the problem. This is why we will never be able to successfully deal with pride until we deal with our insecurity. Our own sense of insecurity and the accompanying feelings of inferiority fuel our prideful behavior.

Insecurity makes us feel that we have to let everyone know who we are and all we've accomplished. That's one reason pride so often manifests itself in bragging. Bragging is really a way of trying to achieve a sense of security and acceptance by making sure that everyone knows exactly how "special" we really are.

If we take a closer look, we can see something lying behind this sense of insecurity. It is fear—fear that people won't accept us or value us unless they know how great we are. So we talk about ourselves in the hopes of being considered worthy of acceptance by others.

There is a fatal flaw in our logic, however. Our accomplishments, no matter how impressive, are not what make us valuable. Even our dreams from God, as wonderful and awe-inspiring as they might be, are not who we are.

As born-again believers, we are blood-washed sons and daughters of the King—that is our true identity. That is "who we are." We must become comfortable and secure in that identity. And when we do, pride and insecurity will no longer have power over us.

I don't know if you've noticed this, but the President of the United States does not feel a need to tell people that he is the president. Think about it. Can you imagine the president walking into a room and announcing, "Hey, pay attention, I'm the President! Commander-in Chief! Leader of the Free World! Yes, sir, 'Mr. President,' they call me."

No. He knows he is the president—so he doesn't have to tell anybody who he is.

Do you realize that Jesus didn't have to tell anybody who He was, either? Jesus knew exactly who He was. But when Satan tempted Jesus in the wilderness, the first thing Satan did was try to create insecurity about His identity (see Matt. 4:1-3). The first thing that Satan said to Him was, "*If* You are the Son of God" (Matt. 4:3, emphasis added); and then Satan tried to tempt Jesus to prove something. But Jesus never even dignified that challenge with a direct answer. Jesus simply replied, "It is written . . . It is written . . . it is written . . ." (Matt. 4:4,7,10).

Jesus could have said, "Oh, yes, I am the Son of God! Just a minute here, Satan! Let me tell you a thing or two about my Son-of-God-ness!" Instead, Jesus set a beautiful example of security. He rested in the simple truth of *His Father's Words*. And that is all that He expects of us when we are tempted with insecurity—to go back to what God our Father has said about us and to rest in that Truth.

Let's explore some of what He has declared about who we are.

Your Identity in Christ

It's vital to understand that the ultimate key to your victory over pride and insecurity is in knowing who you are in Christ.

Jesus knew who He was in His relationship with the Father, so He didn't have to prove anything about Himself. In the same way, we must come to a place where our identities are in Christ and in our relationship *with* Him—not in what we do *for* Him. If our identity is in what we do, or the name that we've built for ourselves, we are failing the Pride Test.

So how can we root out insecurity and prevent pride from thriving in our lives? With two powerful weapons—knowing who we are and remembering who we were.

First of all, we must know who we are.

In short, we are children of the King, beloved and cherished by the mighty, sovereign Creator of the universe.

It's easy to be secure, because we know our heavenly Father loves us. And it really doesn't matter whether others know that or not. We don't need to brag or tell anyone about it, because we know in our hearts that we're His children, and that is what is really important.

Knowing this—really *knowing* it—is the death of insecurity. But what about pride? Can the seeds from its flower still clutter our hearts? How can we be sure that we are never again tempted to be prideful?

The way we must deal with pride is to remind ourselves of who we used to be, to remember that we were adopted. You see, although we are fully children of the King, we know we weren't born in the palace. Rather, we came into the world as beggars—mere peasants in the village. But the King looked out of the window of His castle and fell in love with us. Then He left the castle and lived as a pauper in the village in order to win our hearts. And when He had won our hearts, He adopted us and took us back to His castle to live as His beloved children forever.

Yes, we are secure in Him. We don't have to tell anyone who we are, because we live in the palace now—and we are children of the King. We know that we are His beloved children, and we can be secure in that for all eternity.

But we also can have victory over pride, because we know what we used to be. Without Him, we were nothing. Jesus declared it to us in John 15:5 when He said, "Apart from me you can do nothing" *(NIV)*.

There is a wonderful sense of security in knowing these two truths. It is liberating to be in a room full of strangers and not feel the need to tell them what you've done or who you are.

When we pass the Pride Test, we can be a "nobody" or do "nothing" and still be confident, content and at peace—because the greatest joy in our lives comes from knowing Him.

If God continues to use us to speak to people, that's great. And if He uses someone else to a greater degree, that is wonderful, too, because our greatest joy is not in proving what we can do for God—*it is in receiving all that He has already done for us.* It is in knowing Him and allowing Him to work in our lives, helping us to fulfill the roles He has given us.

Abiding in the Truth

I have found a very easy method for keeping these truths fresh every day: I spend time with God.

It is easy to be humble when you've stood a while in the presence of a holy God. If you walk into your prayer closet in the morning and meet with God, it is very difficult to come out of that meeting with pride! When you meet with God, you see how big He is, how wonderful He is and how awesome He is. You are reminded of the fact that it has only been because of His grace that you have come this far. You walk out of that meeting knowing exactly who you are—and Whose you are.

This is the way to pass, and keep on passing, the Pride Test. It's also the best way to discover God's dream for you. If you're not sure about God's highest and best for your life, I can tell you the best way to find out. Get to know God! Get to know the One who is the Creator of the dream. Spend time with Him.

Then he said, "Hear now My words: If there is a prophet among you, I, the LORD, make Myself known to him in a vision; I speak to him in a dream. Not so with My servant Moses; he is faithful in all My house. I speak with him face to face, even plainly, and not in dark sayings; and he sees the form of the LORD. Why then were you not afraid to speak against My servant Moses?" (Num. 12:6-8).

This Scripture states that God spoke to Moses "face to face" and "plainly," (v. 8) because Moses "[was] faithful in all My house" (v. 7). In other words, because Moses was seeking God first, God spoke to him as a friend. Moses was not seeking the dream, and he was not seeking the destiny. He was seeking a relationship with God; he was seeking God's presence first. And because of that, God said that He would reveal Himself to Moses "face to face" (v. 8).

Moses understood that there is something much more important than knowing God's dream for your life. It is knowing God. So if you're not certain of what God has dreamed for your life, I want to encourage you—don't pursue the dream, but pursue the Giver of the dream. Pursue the One who not only will reveal the dream to you but will also bring it to pass. When you get to know God as a friend, God will speak to you. He will reveal His dream for you. And then He will give you the ability to carry it out.

Discerning Which Dreams Are from God

I have to say this before we go any further: You may be holding on to some dreams that are not from God. We all have had some dreams, perhaps from our childhood, that are really just worldly fantasies. For example, remember when you played the saxophone in high school? You had big dreams of becoming a famous jazz musician. Well, I hate to be the one to break the news to you, but that record company probably isn't going to call!

At one time or another we will have to let go of those fantasies in order to fully embrace the dreams that God has given us.

So, how can we know which dreams are from God? The only way is to get to know Him. Spend time with Him—get to know Him as a friend. As we get to know the Lord, as we make a habit of speaking to Him heart to heart, He reveals His deepest thoughts to us. It is then that He lets us know the dreams that He has for us.

On a personal note, I truly believe that I am stepping into the destiny God has for my life. As I walk on the path that God has chosen for me, I realize that God's destiny is far better than the destiny I thought I had. That's why it's not hard for me to let go of anything that isn't really part of His plan. I've come to understand that God's dreams for us are much better than any dream we could dream for ourselves. God's destiny for us is much bigger than anything we can imagine. The more we seek to know Him, the more this realization will seep into our hearts and minds.

And as we press in to knowing God, He will show us who we really are in Him. He will help us understand the security that we have as His sons and daughters.

Then we can pass the Pride Test—and move on to discover the wondrous destiny that He has prepared for each one of us.

CHAPTER TWO

THE
PIT TEST

I once heard a story about a man who had an unfortunate experience on his walk home from work one night. This man worked late into the night, and his shift didn't end until the wee hours of the morning. In order to get home more quickly, he usually took a shortcut across a cemetery.

One moonless night he couldn't see very well, and he happened to fall into a grave that had been dug the previous day. Try as he might, he couldn't get himself out of that hole. So he began to shout and throw dirt and rocks, in the hopes that someone would come and rescue him. But it was the middle of the night, and no one was around to hear his cries for help. Finally he decided to just wait until morning, when someone was bound to come by and help him. So he just sat down quietly in the corner of the grave.

Later that evening a drunk was walking across the cemetery, and he happened to fall into the same freshly dug grave. Try as he might, he couldn't get himself out of that hole. So, like the first man, he began to shout for help and throw rocks—but all was dark and quiet, and he received no response. Then, suddenly, a hand seemed to come from out of nowhere and touch him on the shoulder. A voice said, "Hey, buddy, there's no getting out of here."

But strangely enough—he did!

That's just an old joke, but it demonstrates the truth that we can accomplish a lot if we are properly motivated. And when you find yourself in "the pits" of life, it's good to know what you can do to get yourself out.

The Pit Test: Finding Your Way Out

Like it or not, all of us will go through some times when we feel as if things are just the pits. We may not be sure just how we got into that pit—and even less sure as to how to get ourselves out. But one thing is certain—we won't move ahead into our destiny unless we get out of that pit! So when I say Joseph was going through the Pit Test, we can all relate to his experience.

That is literally the situation in which Joseph found himself, just after receiving those glorious dreams from God. Everything had seemed to be going so well for Joseph. Then suddenly he was in a pit (see Gen. 37:24), and it seemed that those dreams of honor and authority were just some kind of cruel joke.

What could have caused Joseph to end up in a pit? And what lessons would he have to learn before he could get out? Like Joseph, it is important for us to understand the lessons of the Pit Test, so we can pass that test and move on.

From Joseph's point of view, that day probably had gotten off to a splendid start. He had recently let his father know that his brothers could use a little improvement in their behavior—and now his father was actually sending him on a mission to go check on them. It may have seemed to Joseph that his dream of leading his family was already being fulfilled. Genesis 37:12-24 tells the story.

Then his brothers went to feed their father's flock in Shechem. And Israel said to Joseph, "Are not your brothers feeding the flock in Shechem? Come, I will send you to them." So he said to him, "Here I am." Then he said to him, "Please go and see if it is well with your brothers and well with the flocks, and bring back word to me." So he sent him out of the Valley of Hebron, and he went to Shechem. Now a certain man found him, and there he was, wandering in the field. And the man asked him, saying, "What are you seeking?" So he said, "I am seeking my brothers. Please tell me where they are feeding their flocks." And the man said, "They have departed from here, for I heard them say, 'Let us go to Dothan.'"

I find it a bit amusing that Joseph was sent out to find his brothers, but then he himself ended up "wandering in the field" (see Gen. 37:15). We know that his brothers called him "this dreamer" (see Gen. 37:19)—and now it appears that he may have been a daydreamer as well. After all, he didn't find the man, the man found him. Now Joseph was only 17, so he may have been easily distracted with his dreaming. But whatever Joseph was dreaming about that day, I have a feeling that he wasn't imagining what was about to happen!

So Joseph went after his brothers and found them in Dothan. Now when they saw him afar off, even before he came near them, they conspired against him to kill him. Then they said to one another, "Look, this dreamer is coming! Come therefore, let us now kill him and cast him into some pit; and we shall say, 'Some wild beast has devoured him.' We shall see what will become of his dreams!" But Reuben heard it, and he delivered him out of their hands, and said, "Let us not kill him." And Reuben said to them, "Shed no blood, but cast him into this pit which is in the wilderness, and do not lay a hand on him"—that he might deliver him out of their hands, and bring him back to his father. So it came to pass, when Joseph had come to his brothers, that they stripped Joseph of his tunic, the tunic of many colors that was on him. Then they took him and cast him into a pit. And the pit was empty; there was no water in it (Gen. 37:17-24).

What a shock! Everything had seemed to be going so well for Joseph up to that point. He was out on a mission to report on his brothers. His father had sent him, and he was even wearing the beautiful coat that marked him as the father's favored son. But before he had known what was happening, he was thrown into a pit! His father was nowhere in sight. He no longer had the beautiful coat his father had given him. He didn't even have food or water in that pit. What was worse, there seemed to be no way out. He might very well die there.

In a very short time, it began to look as though his dreams were never going to come to pass. Joseph was going through the Pit Test.

All of us must endure this particular test at one time or another. We experience the Pit Test when nothing in our lives seems to go right. It is when things that were going along smoothly suddenly seem to go very wrong all at once. And it is during the Pit Test that it is easy for us to get discouraged and depressed—because when we are in a pit, it appears there is no way out.

Every one of us is going to fall into a pit at some time in our lives. The question is, Are we going to stay in that pit forever? Or are we going to pass the Pit Test and move on into our destiny?

If we want to know how to get out of the pits of life, it is important to understand how it is that we fall into them. There are reasons that we end up in a pit—and there are tests we must pass to get out of it.

Reasons You Find Yourself in the "Pit"

First of all, we need to recognize that some pits are just a part of life. In John 16:33 Jesus said, "In the world you *will* have tribulation [or trouble]" (emphasis added).

Jesus knew we would have trouble because He knew we would be living in a world contaminated by the effects of sin. As a consequence of sin, this world is full of trouble—and pits are just one form it. Pits are simply a by-product of a fallen world.

Now, we can invite that trouble ourselves (and often do), or trouble can just decide to show up uninvited! Either way, in the course of life, we can expect to encounter some trouble. As long as we are on this earth, we will go through some difficult situations, some challenging times.

Oftentimes when we find ourselves in a pit, it seems that we have had very little to do with how we got there. But if we look inward, we usually find that we have played at least some part in getting ourselves into a pit—and all too often we don't recognize our own responsibility. In difficult times it is much easier to blame others than it is to take a good, hard look at ourselves. And because the world is full of sin, there's certainly never a shortage of other people to blame!

In difficult times it is much easier to blame others than it is to take a good, hard look at ourselves.

It has become very popular in our society today to adopt a victim mentality—in other words, to blame all of our problems on other people. If we are going through a difficult time, it's easy to blame our trouble or failure on our parents, our spouse or even the government.

I don't wish to sound harsh or insensitive, but if your parents dropped you on your head when you were a baby, I'm sorry, but it's time to get over it! If you're 48 years old now, it's time to move past this incident and do something with your life. That is an extreme example, but I'm trying to make an important point: Even if the sins of others have put you into a pit, you are the only one who can take responsibility to get out of it. And you will never get out until you stop blaming other people for the difficulties you encounter in life.

Joseph had the perfect opportunity to develop a victim mentality. After all, he was just trying to obey his father when his brothers threw him into the pit. And we know his brothers did it out of jealousy, because the Scriptures state clearly that his brothers not only envied him but hated him as well (see Gen. 37:4,11). So it would have been easy to put all the blame for the pit incident onto Joseph's brothers. It would have been easy for Joseph to focus only on their sins and never take a good look at his own pride.

It's true that Joseph's brothers had an evil attitude—and that attitude prompted them to throw Joseph in the pit. But Joseph also had a sinful attitude, which contributed to the problem. Joseph had an attitude of pride.

In Genesis 37:18 it says: "Now when they saw him afar off, even before he came near them, they conspired against him to kill him." Think about that for a moment. How do you suppose they were able to see that it was Joseph from such a great distance? I believe they were able to see him because he was wearing that coat of many colors. It may have been orange, green, yellow or purple for all we know. But whatever it looked like, it was probably visible from far away.

I'm sure Joseph loved that coat and wore it everywhere he went. His father had given it to him as a sign of his favor, so it's understandable that the coat would be special to him. But we know Joseph had a problem with pride. And it is possible, even likely, that Joseph wore that coat with an *attitude* of pride, causing his brothers to feel even more envious.

His brothers were out in the wilderness taking care of the sheep, working hard for their father—and from a mile away they could see that coat coming. That may have made them angry, especially if they felt that Joseph was always showing off. Perhaps Joseph was always projecting the attitude, "I'm my father's favorite. I'm the best one. I'm better than all of you."

If you think about it, why were Joseph's brothers together, working in the field, while Joseph stayed at home? Many theologians believe that his father had to separate them, because Joseph's brothers hated him so much—his bragging created too much conflict. Jacob may have sent Joseph out to find them in the hopes that some reconciliation could take place, since it's not likely that Jacob really wanted Joseph to check on his brothers' well-being. After all, they were 10 grown men, all professionals and all older than Joseph. Jacob probably knew the brothers were all right—he was just trying to help a relationship develop between Joseph and them. But Joseph was such a braggart that the relationship between his brothers and him had become terribly strained.

Further, Joseph shared some responsibility for creating that strained relationship and making it worse. Joseph may have looked like an innocent victim in that pit, but he had contributed to the events that put him there.

I've heard similar stories from individuals who believe their problems are strictly the result of the attitudes of others. "People are just jealous of me," they will say. "I'm not the one who has a problem. It's not the way that I act; it's not the way that I talk; it's not the way I present myself. Everyone else has the problem!"

When we find ourselves in a pit, we first need to take a good look at ourselves. We need to consider that we are the problem and that we are the reason we are in the pit. It's true that Joseph's brothers had a problem, an envy problem. But Joseph had a problem, too—a pride problem. And that pride was the real reason Joseph ended up in the pit. The source of his problems was within his own heart.

We can learn a lot about the Pit Test by seeing ourselves in Joseph. Joseph was a son who had his father's favor. In much the same way, we are sons and daughters of the King, and we also have the favor of our heavenly Father. Reflect on Psalm 5:12: "For You, O LORD, will bless the righteous; with favor You will surround him as with a shield."

Joseph's father, out of his great love for him, had given him a gift. In much the same way, our heavenly Father gives gifts to us—and He doesn't take them back.

But Joseph became proud of the gift his father gave him, and he showed it off every chance he got. He started to find his identity in the *gift* that identified him as the favored son, rather than in the *relationship* that made him the favored son. He ended up losing that gift as a result.

In much the same way, we can become caught up in the gifts God has given us. We can start to find our identity or sense of worth in that gift, rather than in the One who gave it. When we do, we become prideful. And we risk losing the gift.

I want to clarify something important. Joseph's father gave him the gift, but *it was not his father who took it away from him.* Joseph lost his coat of many colors through his own actions. He lost it because he was prideful about it and what it represented.

When God gives us gifts, He doesn't take them back. The Bible tells us the gifts and callings of God are irrevocable—the *King James Version* says they are "without repentance" (Rom. 11:29). This means God does not take back the gifts He has given us. But we can lose them ourselves if we walk in pride. I wonder how many people have a gift from God, but they are not able to use it because they walk in pride?

What if that happens? What if we lose the gift of God through our own actions? Is there any hope for getting it back?

To answer that, I want you to think about the end of Joseph's story. Joseph ended up becoming the governor of Egypt, the second most powerful man in the world. As a consequence of that, he also became the second richest man in the world. He probably had hundreds of coats of many colors, as many coats as his heart could desire. So God restored what he had lost a hundredfold.

And Joseph got back something much more important than a coat. He got back his relationship with his father. For years he didn't have fellowship with his father—he wasn't even sure if he was alive. But after Joseph had learned to walk in humility, God restored his relationship with his father—as well as everything else he had lost.

When you find yourself in a pit, you may feel that all is lost. But if you cry out to God in humility of heart, He is eager to restore you. The Bible says that if you humble yourself, you will be exalted (see 1 Pet. 5:6).

Whatever you have lost, God can replace it a hundredfold if you repent and walk in humility.

Lies of the Pit

We've learned that it is dangerous to walk in pride, because you can end up in a pit. But we need to understand that the pit itself can also be a dangerous place. That is because of what I call the lies of the pit.

Be assured, any time you fall into a pit you will encounter the lies of the enemy—lies of accusation, lies of hopelessness, even fabricated evidence. And if you believe his lies, you could stay in that pit indefinitely.

If you want to get out of that pit, you are going to have to learn to discern the enemy's lies and resist them with the Truth.

The first truth we must keep in mind in order to overcome the lies of the pit is this: It is Satan who accuses us, not God. Revelation 12:10 identifies Satan as *"the accuser of our brethren"* (emphasis added). So any time you have a thought that is accusatory, know it is from Satan.

This is important to understand, because when you fall into a pit, the devil will immediately begin to accuse you. You can hear his accusations in your mind, in your thoughts. Satan introduces thoughts like, *See, you're no good, or you wouldn't be in this pit. What's more, you'll never be any good. You'll never do anything for God. You'll never get your marriage straightened out. You'll never get your life straightened out.* Every time you hear a thought like that in your mind, remind yourself of the source. Because it is Satan who accuses us, not God—and we are commanded to resist him (see Jas. 4:7).

There is a difference between being accused by the enemy and being convicted by the Holy Spirit. You can recognize conviction of the Holy Spirit because the Spirit always offers hope. Conviction says, "You did this wrong; but if you repent, I'll make it right and help you overcome it." But condemnation says, "You always do things wrong. You'll never do anything right. You'll never get better. Things will never work out for you." Condemnation is not from God.

When Joseph was in the pit, he had the opportunity to be accused by the enemy and believe his lies. Satan probably came to Joseph and said, "It is over, man. Those dreams you had are never going to come to pass. You've blown it too thoroughly with that pride thing, and now it's simply too late. You're going to die in this pit. Everything is over. There is no reason to call out to God now. And why should you trust God anyway? After all, look what God let happen to you. He doesn't really care about you. Actually, He never did."

That is what the enemy does. Every time we're in a pit, Satan is right there to accuse us. And he doesn't stop there. He accuses God as well. He says, "Look at what God did to you. Look at what God let happen to you. God is not faithful to you. If He were faithful, this never would have happened."

Joseph had to fight against the lies of the enemy, and so must we—if we want to get out of the pit. We know God is faithful. We know His words are true. But when we are in the pit, the enemy will try to get us to focus on our circumstances, rather than on God's faithfulness. The enemy will even manipulate those circumstances to try to make his lies look like the truth. So if we let the circumstances determine what we believe, we can be caught in the lies of the pit.

When we are in the pit, the enemy will try to get us to focus on our circumstances, rather than on God's faithfulness.

It is important to understand this, because the enemy is very deceptive. He will not only tell you a lie, he will also *fabricate evidence* to support his lies. This is how he was able to get Joseph's father to believe the lie that Joseph was dead.

> So they took Joseph's tunic, killed a kid of the goats, and dipped the tunic in the blood. Then they sent the tunic of many colors, and they brought it to their father and said, "We have found this. Do you know whether it is your son's tunic or not?" And he recognized it and said, "It is my son's tunic. A wild beast has devoured him. Without doubt Joseph is torn to pieces" (Gen. 37:31-33).

The brothers didn't actually tell their father that Joseph had been devoured by wild animals. Instead, they created false evidence and then asked their father a misleading question—"Is this your son's coat?" Jacob believed that evidence, and he jumped to the conclusion that his son was dead. Out of his own mouth Jacob said, "My son has been killed by wild animals." But it was a lie—and he believed that lie for more than 20 years.

Think about it. For 22 years Jacob believed his son was dead. For 22 years he probably cried himself to sleep at night, with nightmares about a lion killing his son, ripping him limb from limb. The Bible says Jacob was so full of grief that he refused to be comforted, and said, "For I shall go down into the grave to my son in mourning" (Gen. 37:35). But it was not true that Joseph was dead. Jacob concluded that it was the truth *based on fabricated evidence.*

Notice the callousness of Joseph's brothers. They heard their father's wailing and they saw his grief. Yet they never went to him with the truth that would have ended his grieving. They could have taken away their father's suffering in an instant by telling him, "Listen, it's not true. Joseph wasn't really torn by wild beasts. We just fabricated that bloody coat." But they never refuted the lie that had been so cleverly planted. Do you see the hardness of their hearts? That is the hardness of sin. This is how deceptive the enemy is.

We live in a sin-hardened world, and we will be tempted by fabricated evidence just as Jacob was. And like Jacob, we will suffer unnecessary grief if we allow the lies of the pit to determine what we believe.

This is very important. If you want to get out of the pit, you must learn to discern the lies of the enemy. Because when you are in the pit, you are especially vulnerable. When you are in the pit, circumstances usually don't look very favorable—and that is exactly when Satan will manipulate those circumstances in order to deceive you. He will hold up those circumstances before you as evidence that you should believe him rather than have faith in God. But fabricated evidence is not the truth. Joseph's brothers held up a bloody coat as evidence, and that evidence looked pretty convincing. But it was fabricated evidence. It was not the truth.

If you want to overcome the lies of the pit, you must learn to focus on what God has said. When you are in the pit, you must remember that nothing is too hard for God, no matter what evidence the enemy might produce.

Let's say you're going through some challenges in your marriage—Satan will fabricate evidence to convince you that you're married to the wrong person. Today psychologists administer personality tests to show that certain partners aren't compatible and should not be married to each other. Yet if you took one of these tests, the evidence could easily tell you a lie. You might look at the test results and say, "Goodness gracious, I'm the opposite of my wife! I guess I'm just married to the wrong person." (Of course you are the opposite of your wife! You wouldn't want to marry someone like you—because if you were married to you, you'd go crazy!)

The truth is that when two people who are opposites come together, God can do a beautiful thing—because together they can look like Jesus. That is God's plan for marriage—to smooth the rough edges so that together you look like Jesus. Yet when those rough edges start to manifest, things can get uncomfortable. And that is when Satan will be right there to lie about God's plan for marriage. He will say, "See, this marriage is never going to work." And then he will produce evidence to support his lie—but it is still a lie. And you will have to resist it.

Yet even worse than his fabricated evidence is Satan's biggest lie: "You've messed up too badly. It's too late for you. You've messed up too badly to ever fulfill God's destiny for your life."

Do you realize that the Bible is a book entirely about restoration? The Bible is filled with stories about people who messed up so badly that it seemed even God couldn't do anything about it—and yet He restored every one of them. He wants you to know that nothing is impossible for Him. As long as you have breath, it is never too late to call out to God. It doesn't matter what pit you are in. If you call out to God, He can fix it. And that call for help is the real purpose of the pit.

The Purpose of the Pit

We can gain some important insight from another Bible character who messed up and got thrown into a pit. His name was Jonah. Remember him? God had a big destiny in mind for Jonah. God gave him an assignment to save an entire city from destruction (see Jonah 1:2). But when

God commanded him to go to Nineveh, Jonah decided to go in the opposite direction (see Jonah 1:3). (Incidentally, this is always a bad strategy!)

So Jonah ended up in the maritime version of a pit—the belly of a fish. "Then Jonah prayed to the LORD his God from the fish's belly. And he said: "I cried out to the LORD because of my affliction, and He answered me. Out of the belly of Sheol I cried, and You heard my voice" (Jonah 2:1-2).

"Sheol" is simply an Old Testament word for "the pit." So Jonah cried out to God from the bottom of the pit.

It shouldn't surprise us that Jonah ended up in a pit. He had messed up pretty badly. God had given Jonah a very important assignment, and Jonah basically had refused to do it. Jonah had run away from God's plans—and as a result, he ended up in the pit. But from the bottom of that pit, Jonah cried out to God. And when he cried out to God, God heard his voice and delivered him.

That is the purpose of the pit.

It is to get us to cry out to God. The purpose of the pit is to get us in a place that is so far down we can't get ourselves out of it—a place where we can't do it on our own. And when we realize we can't do it on our own, we will cry out to God.

I want you to know that no matter what pit you're in—even if you dug it yourself—God is big enough to get you out of it!

It's not a hard thing for God to get you out of a pit. He is a redeeming God, and He actually delights in getting His children out of pits. It doesn't matter how many pits you might be in. You could even be in several pits at the same time. You might be in a pit test with your finances, a pit test with your marriage and a pit test with your job. But God can deliver you out of every one of them, if you'll just call out to Him.

The most important question is not whether God can deliver you out of the pit. The most important question is whether you are going to call out to God in humility—or are you going to simply gripe, murmur and complain?

I hate to point this out, but much of what we like to call prayer is nothing more than complaining. Just because we are "talking" to God, we think of it as prayer—but it really isn't talking to God as if He were our loving Father. It's griping to Him about everything we don't like.

I'm sure Joseph was tempted to gripe when he found himself in his pit. It's not hard to imagine him pacing back and forth in the pit, murmuring to God about how unfair it all was: "God, why would You let this happen to me? After all, I'm such a good and upright person. I have such a destiny on my life. I just can't believe You would let this happen to me!"

I'll bet the first part of Joseph's conversation was like that—just griping.

But somewhere in that pit Joseph must have changed. Somewhere in that pit, Joseph must have cried out to God in true humility—because after the experience in the pit, Joseph was a changed man. Joseph may have failed the first test, but he went on to take nine other tests in his life. And from that point on, he started to do the right thing every time. It is actually amazing to see how many times Joseph did the right thing when he was faced with a temptation.

Something happened to Joseph in that pit. Somewhere in that pit Joseph must have taken responsibility for his own sins and failures. Somewhere in that pit Joseph must have cried out to God in true humility. Somewhere in that pit Joseph must have knelt and said, "God, I need You to forgive me. I admit that I'm a prideful, arrogant person—and I ask You to do a work in my heart."

When Joseph did that, his situation began to change. Although it wasn't apparent at the time, circumstances began to line up in the direction of his destiny. First his brother Judah got the idea to sell Joseph to Midianite traders, rather than leave him in the pit to die (see Gen. 37:26-28). And those Midianite traders brought Joseph to Egypt and sold him to Potiphar (see Gen. 37:36). Now being sold as a slave might not seem like a great alternative to the pit, but it was better than certain death—and Joseph certainly would have died if he had been left in the pit.

Before Joseph ever got into that pit, God had a plan to get him out, and bring him into his destiny. And when Joseph cried out to God, God began working through that situation, because being sold as a slave in Egypt brought Joseph one step closer to his destiny. Joseph's brothers meant it for evil, but God meant it for good (see Gen. 50:20).

Redemption from the Pit

God always has a plan. No matter what pit we might be in, God has a plan to get us out of it. And if we dig a little deeper in this story, we can see some types and shadows of God's master plan of redemption. His ultimate plan was to redeem us through His Son Jesus Christ. And there are types, or images, of Jesus in this story.

Remember, Joseph's brothers hadn't really wanted to throw him into a pit. Their original plan was to kill him! But Joseph's oldest brother Reuben intervened.

> And Reuben said to them, "Shed no blood, but cast him into this pit which is in the wilderness, and do not lay a hand on him"—that he might deliver him out of their hands, and bring him back to his father (Gen. 37:22).

Now if anyone had a right to be jealous of Joseph, it was Reuben, because Reuben was the firstborn son—and the firstborn was the one on whom the honor should have rested. But Reuben gave up that honor for Joseph's sake. In this situation with Joseph, Reuben had two purposes as the firstborn son: He wanted to *deliver* Joseph, and he wanted *to bring him back to his father*.

In this way Reuben was a type of the Lord Jesus Christ. Jesus is the firstborn Son of God, the One on whom God's favor rests. But Jesus gave up all those rights and privileges so that you and I could become God's favored sons and daughters. Jesus left the glories of heaven with a twofold purpose: to deliver us and to bring us back to His Father. So Reuben is a type of Christ.

Joseph is also a type of Christ.

Joseph was stripped of his robe of many colors (see Gen. 37:23). Jesus was stripped of His robe, and soldiers gambled for it (see Matt. 27:28,35).

Joseph was sold for 20 pieces of silver (see Gen. 37:26-28). Jesus was sold for 30 pieces of silver (see Matt. 26:14-15). (Joseph was sold for 20 pieces of silver to the Midianite traders. But they took Joseph to Egypt and sold him at a profit. The price of a slave at that time was 30 pieces of silver. So history indicates that Joseph was ultimately sold for 30 pieces of silver, too).[1]

Joseph was betrayed by Judah (see Gen. 37:26-27). Jesus was betrayed by Judas (see Matt. 26:25). ("Judah" and "Judas" are the same word in Hebrew.)

The Midianite traders who brought Joseph to Egypt were carrying spices, balm and myrrh (see Gen. 37:25). The disciple Nicodemus brought myrrh and aloes to the tomb to embalm the body of Jesus (see John 19:39).

Joseph was thrown into a pit, and then God delivered him out of that pit. Jesus was in the grave for three days, and then God raised him up.

But there is a very important difference between Jesus and Joseph: *Jesus didn't do anything to deserve being thrown into that pit.*

Rather, we deserved to have been thrown into the pit. We sinned, and we should have been thrown into the pit for all eternity. But Jesus Christ went to the pit for us, so we would never have to go there. He spent three days in "Sheol," so we wouldn't have to spend eternity in hell. Jesus did it willingly for you and for me—and God didn't leave Him there in that pit.

Psalm 16:10 says, "For You will not leave my soul in Sheol, nor will You allow Your Holy One to see corruption." This was a Messianic prophecy about Jesus—a prophecy that was fulfilled. God did not leave His only begotten Son in a pit. And He will not leave you in a pit either.

If you are in a pit right now, and it looks like there is no way out, I have good news: Jesus Christ has been there before you. Our Lord and Savior went to the pit for you—and then God raised Him up from that pit, as the firstborn of many brothers and sisters.

Jesus Christ died to deliver you from every pit. He died so that you might have life. Receive what Jesus did for you. He came to deliver you and to bring you back to the Father.

You may have walked away from the gift God gave you by walking in pride. God can restore that gift a hundredfold, if you'll simply call out to Him. Just do what Joseph did; do what Jonah did. Cry out to God from that pit. Say, "God, I'm sorry. I've walked in pride."

And when you humble yourself and cry out to God, He will deliver you out of every pit. He will promote you beyond the pit, and He will exalt you so that you might walk in the destiny He has planned.

CHAPTER THREE

THE PALACE TEST

M y tires screeched a little as I hurried my car around a tight corner at the airport parking garage. Debbie and I were running late, and there wasn't a moment to lose if we were going to catch our flight.

I breathed a little prayer of thanks as I spotted an open parking space.

As I tried to fit into that spot, I forgot to take into account a trailer hitch that we had just put on the week before. The trailer hitch was sticking out just the "wrong" amount; and I as I backed up, it hit the bumper of the car behind me. Just what we didn't need at that moment! I jumped out to investigate, only to see that the impact had just barely damaged the plastic on the other vehicle's bumper.

What to do? Certainly the right thing to do was to leave a note—but taking the time to do so would certainly cause us to miss our flight. I hate to admit this, but I couldn't help noticing that the car was old and had quite a few dings, dents and scratches. *The dented plastic would hardly be noticeable*, I rationalized. I was in a dilemma, so I made a decision. I told myself that the damaged plastic probably wouldn't have any effect on the owner of that car—but missing our flight would certainly have a *big* effect on us and on our plans.

"We've got to get to that plane!" I announced, and I then headed toward the terminal. But I hadn't gotten very far when a still, small voice spoke up inside me.

"Is that really worth it?" the voice asked. "Is catching a plane so important that it's worth forfeiting the favor of God?"

I stopped in my tracks, turned to Debbie and said, "I'm sorry, Honey. I just have to leave a note."

"I know," Debbie said, her voice a mixture of pride and relief. "I knew you would."

"We're probably going to miss our flight, you know."

"I know," she replied, without a hint of misgiving.

So I wrote a note and left it on the damaged car, with my phone number and apologies. We did end up missing our flight, but we were able to line up a later one. So we went to lunch, enjoyed each other's company for a while and took the later flight.

The Palace Test: Learning Good Stewardship

What had seemed so important at the time was really just a temporary inconvenience. In retrospect, it seems ridiculous that I could have looked upon that inconvenience as more serious than the consequences of not doing the right thing. Because Jesus said that if I am unfaithful in a small thing, or that which is "least," then He will rightly assume that I will also be unfaithful in "much." And a person whom God cannot trust with much is a person who will have to wait a long time to enter into his or her destiny.

Jesus talked about this in Luke 16:10-12:

He who is faithful in what is least is faithful also in much; and he who is unjust in what is least is unjust also in much. Therefore if you have not been faithful in the unrighteous mammon, who will commit to your trust the true riches? And if you have not been faithful in what is another man's, who will give you what is your own?

What are you going to do with another man's goods? What are you going to do with those things that have been entrusted to you by God—right down to the pavement you share in a parking lot? This is the test of stewardship, and it is the first test that Joseph encountered after he was delivered out of the pit.

Every one of us would like to move on into a glorious destiny. But as we've already seen, every great destiny carries with it great responsibility. And God will not allow us "to be tempted beyond what [we] are able" (1 Cor. 10:13). So God is watching to see whether we can be trusted with little things, before He will give us those great things He has in store for us.

What will we do with the job He has given us? With the boss He has given us? Will we be faithful with another person's goods—even if that person is an unbeliever? God says this is the test that determines whether He will trust us with *His* goods. So until we pass the test of stewardship, we will never move on into our destiny.

In the book of Colossians, God speaks to us about our roles as servants.

> Bondservants, obey in all things your masters according to the flesh, not with eyeservice, as men-pleasers, but in sincerity of heart, fearing God. And whatever you do, do it heartily, as to the Lord and not to men, knowing that from the Lord you will receive the reward of the inheritance; for you serve the Lord Christ. But he who does wrong will be repaid for what he has done, and there is no partiality (Col. 3:22-25).

God is saying that He wants us to serve our earthly masters with all of our hearts, just as if we were serving Him. And He reminds us that He is the One who will reward us, since it is really Christ Jesus we are serving (see v. 24). So even if you are a "bondservant" (v. 22), even if you are serving an unbelieving boss, God wants you to serve that boss from your heart with all sincerity—because when you do, you are serving "the Lord Christ" (v. 24).

Can you serve someone else well? Can you serve an unbeliever well? Do you work with unbelievers? Can you have a right attitude toward them? If you can't serve unbelievers well, you will never pass the test of stewardship, because God has placed you in that situation as His servant, and He is watching to see if you will faithfully represent Him to the world.

Whatever your job may be, you must understand that you don't only work for your employer—you also work for God. And because you work for God, He will reward you. He will promote you, and He will put His blessing on all that you do.

This is the reason Joseph was promoted everywhere he went. Joseph didn't only work for Potiphar; he didn't only work for the keeper of the prison; and he didn't only work for Pharaoh. Joseph also always worked for the Lord, whatever his circumstances were. And because Joseph worked "heartily, as to the Lord" (v. 23), God blessed him.

It wasn't very long after Joseph was delivered out of the pit that he found himself living in a palace. And soon afterward Joseph was given rule over almost everything in that palace. Yet he had to remember that *nothing in that palace belonged to him.* Joseph was only a steward. (And that is why I like to call the test of stewardship the Palace Test!)

Genesis 39 tells the story.

Now Joseph had been taken down to Egypt. And Potiphar, an officer of Pharaoh, captain of the guard, an Egyptian, bought him from the Ishmaelites who had taken him down there. The LORD was with Joseph, and he was a successful man; and he was in the house of his master the Egyptian. And his master saw that the LORD was with him and that the LORD made all he did to prosper in his hand. So Joseph found favor in his sight, and served him. Then he made him overseer of his house, and all that he had he put under his authority. So it was, from the time that he had made him overseer of his house and all that he had, that the LORD blessed the Egyptian's house for Joseph's sake; and the blessing of the LORD was on all that he had in the house and in the field. Thus he left all that he had in Joseph's hand, and he did not know what he had except for the bread which he ate. And Joseph was handsome in form and appearance (Gen. 39:1-6).

Joseph had gone from the pit to the palace pretty quickly. That might sound wonderful, but don't forget that Joseph was still a slave. Although he was put in charge of all Potiphar's goods, he had no promise of a natural reward for doing a good job—not even the minimum wage! Joseph was a slave, and as a slave he had no rights of any kind. Yet we know that Joseph proved himself a faithful guardian of Potiphar's goods—and that he passed the critical test of stewardship. How do we know that?

Look at verse 2 again: "The LORD was with Joseph" and that caused Joseph to be "a successful man." In fact, the presence of God was so obvious on Joseph's life that even his Egyptian master somehow knew that "the LORD was with him" (v. 3). And that tangible presence of God in Joseph's life caused him to have favor with his master. But Joseph did not try to take advantage of his favored status. Rather, God's Word tells us that Joseph "served him" (v. 4).

In other words, Joseph had the right attitude toward his job, even his job as a slave. He didn't allow the injustice of his situation to prevent him from serving his master faithfully. And because of this, Potiphar made Joseph the "overseer of his house and all that he had" (Gen. 39:4). Now this Hebrew word for "overseer" is translated in the Septuagint as the same Greek word that is used in 1 Timothy and Titus to refer to an elder of the church.[1] So Joseph's master actually gave him the position of an "elder" in his house—a pretty high honor to bestow upon a slave.

If you look at verse 23, you can see that Joseph carried this same attitude with him when he was sent to the prison. "The keeper of the prison did not look into anything that was under Joseph's authority, because the LORD was with him; and whatever he did, the LORD made it prosper" (Gen. 39:23).

Once again, Joseph did not allow the injustice of his situation prevent him from being a faithful worker. And because he was such a good steward, "the LORD was with him" (v. 23) in the prison, just as He had been in the palace. So Joseph was made the overseer of the prison as well.

How did Joseph pass the test of stewardship? He passed it by being faithful with another man's goods; by being faithful to do the right thing, even when there seemed to be no reward for doing so. And because of that, God was with Joseph and prospered the work of his hands.

Think about that for just a moment. Whatever Joseph did, the Lord made it prosper. Even the labor that he did as a slave was so blessed by the Lord that it caused the house of his master to prosper—just for Joseph's sake!

Now think about something else for just a moment. Would it be okay if that happened to you? Would it be okay with you if the Lord made whatever you touched prosper? Would you mind if He made your marriage prosper? If He made your children prosper? If He made your job, your health and your relationships prosper? How would you like it if you could be like Joseph and have the Lord make you prosper in everything you do?

The wonderful news is that you *can* be like Joseph. You can learn the keys to being a faithful steward. When you learn these keys, the Lord will be with you as He was with Joseph. And the Lord will cause you to prosper in all that you do.

This is a simple message, but it is so simple that you could easily miss it. You could easily assume that you've heard all of this before. But if you are not prospering in every area of your life, I encourage you to think deeply about the truths I am about to share. Because if you're not prospering in every area of your life, you may not be putting some of these truths into practice.

"Prospering" Is Not a Bad Word

Let's settle something right at the start: "Prospering" is not a bad word! But it seems that every time God restores a truth to the Church, Satan tries to deposit an error. In other words, when God reveals a truth to us, Satan tries to make us abuse that truth and turn it into an error by taking it too far. I believe God tried to restore the truth about biblical prosperity to the Church, but then Satan tempted some people to get greedy in this area. I believe it is possible that Satan even tempted some influential pastors and leaders in the ministry to get out of balance in this area. All of a sudden we had what was labeled the "Prosperity Doctrine"—and because of the errors of a few, "prosperity" was suddenly viewed as a bad word.

But the word "prosperity" is a biblical word; it is not a bad word! Why would you be bothered to know that God wants you to prosper? Why would it bother you to know that a good and loving God wants your marriage to prosper, that He wants your relationship with your children to prosper, that He wants you to be blessed and to be a blessing?

God really does want you to prosper; He really does want you to succeed.

Do not look at the excesses of a few and back away from what the Bible says is true. The Bible says that God really does want you to prosper; He really does want you to succeed. There are so many Scripture passages about prospering that I can't share all of them here—but let me just show you a few.

Take a look at Genesis 26:12-13:

> Then Isaac sowed in that land, and reaped in the same year a hundredfold; and the LORD blessed him. The man began to prosper, and continued prospering until he became very prosperous.

Did you notice that the Lord uses the word "prosper" 3 times in this verse about Isaac? I think God is trying to say something here about prospering! Remember, these are not the words of some man; these words in the Bible have been spoken by God Himself. And He is not afraid to use the word "prosper" or the word "prospered"—or even the word "prosperity." In fact, the Old Testament uses the word "prospering" 63 times!

Or consider these inspiring words from the New Testament:

Beloved, I pray that you may prosper in all things and be in health, just as your soul prospers (3 John 2).

The Hebrew word for "prospering" means "to push forward," or make progress; and the Greek word for "prospering" means "to help on the road."[2] In other words, if you "prosper" other people, you help them along the road. If you "prosper" others, you push them forward; you help them get farther along than they were.

How would you like to have God "push you forward" in your marriage? How would you like to have God "push you forward" in your job? How would you like to say, "No, no, God! Quit pushing! That's enough! I have already been so blessed!" But then God just keeps pushing you forward. Wouldn't that be wonderful?

The great news is that God does want to push you forward, and He wants to help you make progress. He wants to prosper you in everything you do, just as He prospered Joseph.

But it is really up to us whether we are going to walk in the blessing of God and the favor of God as Joseph did.

So what are the keys that caused Joseph to prosper? Let's find out!

The Key to Prospering: The Presence of the Lord

The key to prospering is quite simply this: the presence of the Lord. If God is with you, walking with you as your friend, you are going to prosper—because God prospers in everything He does. Do you realize that God's ventures are always successful? He has never failed at anything that He has done. So if He is with you, you are going to be successful! If God is with you, He is always going to be pushing you forward. If God is with you, you cannot help but be blessed.

So, the key to prospering is simply to have the presence of the Lord in your life.

Joseph had the presence of the Lord on his life in a tangible way. It is amazing to me that Potiphar, who did not know the Lord, was still able to recognize that God was with Joseph: "[Potiphar] saw that the LORD was with him and that the LORD made all he did to prosper in his hand" (Gen. 37:3). Potiphar realized that God's favor rested upon young Joseph.

Does your boss, who may be an unbeliever, recognize that God is with you? Does he recognize that his company is being blessed because you are an employee? That is what this test is all about. Because if God is with you, He will prosper everything you do.

The phrase "The LORD was with him" is found throughout the Bible and is used to describe many other people of faith. It is not unusual for the Lord to bless His servants with His presence. The Lord wants to bless you with His presence, too. And this is the key to prospering—to have the presence of the Lord with you at all times. But that prompts another question.

What is the key to the presence of the Lord?

The Key to the Presence of the Lord: Obedience

I'm afraid that we often don't like the word "obedience" very much. (Oddly enough, we seem to want *other* people to like it.) Whether or not we like the "O" word is not the issue. We cannot escape this simple truth: Obedience is the key to having the presence of God in our lives. If we don't obey God, He can't walk with us. Because of His holy and righteous nature, God walks only with obedient servants.

We see this linkage in 2 Chronicles 17:3-4:

> Now the LORD was with Jehoshaphat, because he walked in the former ways of his father David; he did not seek the Baals, but sought the God of his father, and walked in His commandments and not according to the acts of Israel.

The Bible says God "was with Jehoshaphat" (v. 3). Why? Because he "walked in [God's] commandments" (v. 4)! The Lord was with Jehoshaphat because he walked in God's ways—because he obeyed.

And we are told that Jehoshaphat followed the example of David, who also had lived in the presence of God.

> Now Saul was afraid of David, because the LORD was with him, but had departed from Saul. And David behaved wisely in all his ways, and the LORD was with him (1 Sam. 18:12,14).

The Lord was with David, but He had departed from Saul. Even Saul was aware of this. Was this because God was playing favorites? No, the Bible states quite clearly that the Lord with David because "David behaved wisely in all his ways" (v. 14). In other words, David was obedient to the Lord—and because David was obedient to the Lord, "the LORD was with him" (v. 14).

Why had the Lord departed from Saul? In 1 Samuel 15 we read about how Saul failed to obey the Lord! God had spoken to Saul and given him direct instructions. But Saul refused to do what God had said to do—and then tried to justify his disobedience, rather than repent. So the presence of the Lord departed from him. God does not walk with the disobedient. "'If you are willing and obedient, you shall eat the good of the land; but if you refuse and rebel, you shall be devoured by the sword'; for the mouth of the LORD has spoken" (Isa. 1:19-20).

The Lord says in this passage that if you want to "eat the good of the land" (v. 19)—in other words, if you want to prosper—you must be willing and obedient. Then He also says that if you are *not* willing and obedient—but refuse and rebel—you will *not* prosper but in fact be devoured. That seems pretty straightforward: Refuse to obey and expose yourself to the forces of destruction. Or obey and prosper!

Notice that God says that we must be *willing* and *obedient* in order to prosper. Clearly our *attitudes* are just as important to God as our *actions*. He wants us to obey Him—and He wants us to do it with a willing heart.

Is it possible to be obedient and yet not be willing? Just ask the parent of a teenager who has been told to clean her room before she will be allowed to go out. If you've ever heard the angry stomping around that sometimes goes with the cleaning, you can imagine the way some of our obedience appears to the Lord.

He wants us to obey Him—but He wants us to do it with a willing heart. And the reason is that *our hearts are what He really wants*. This is precisely what we're told in 2 Chronicles: "For the eyes of the LORD move to and fro throughout the earth that He may strongly support those whose heart is completely His" (2 Chron. 16:9, *NASB*).

He wants *us*, not just some outward act. And if we want Him—if we want His presence in our lives—we must obey Him, and obey Him wholeheartedly. It's a choice!

> Behold, I set before you today a blessing and a curse: the blessing, if you obey the commandments of the LORD your God which I command you today; and the curse, if you do not obey the commandments of the LORD your God, but turn aside from the way which I command you today, to go after other gods which you have not known (Deut. 11:26-28).

God has set before us a blessing and a curse. The choice is really very simple. And this is the choice God has given us: "If you obey Me, you will be blessed. If you disobey Me, you will not be blessed."

The blessing of God comes through obedience.

Please understand, God is not talking about our salvation here. Salvation is not by works but by grace which comes through faith in the atoning blood of Jesus Christ. But in this verse God is talking about *being blessed in this life*. He is letting us know that we can choose to be blessed or cursed during our time on this earth. And if we choose to obey His commands, we have chosen the blessing: "If they obey and serve Him, they shall spend their days in prosperity, and their years in pleasures. But if they do not obey, they shall perish by the sword, and they shall die without knowledge" (Job 36:11-12).

Would you like to spend your days in prosperity, and your years in pleasure? Then obey God and serve Him.

Let me emphasize again that this is not a doctrine of works. This is a doctrine of *obedience*. We know that salvation is the free gift of God—but we must understand that the *blessing* of God comes through obedience. And this is so because our obedience to God is the truest indication that our hearts truly belong to Him.

Jehoshaphat, David and Joseph walked in obedience to God. As a result, God was with them. They showed their love toward God by obeying Him with willing hearts—and He blessed their lives with His presence. Likewise, if we show God our love by obeying Him with willing hearts, God's presence will be with us!

Please understand that I am not talking about the omnipresence of God—His presence that is in every place at every time. Every person in this world—every believer, every nonbeliever—is in the omnipresence of God. Even the rocks and the stones are always in God's presence, since He is everywhere. But as believers, that is not the kind of presence of God we want to settle for—God has invited us to true intimacy with Him.

Nor am I talking about the inward presence of God. When you become born again, the Holy Spirit comes to live inside your heart by faith. This is the inner presence of God. And it is a wonderful thing to have the Holy Spirit of the living God come and take up His abode within you.

But there is something more: the manifest presence of God. This is when God comes in a tangible way and makes His presence known. I'm sure almost every believer has experienced that special sweetness that sometimes fills the atmosphere during times of worship and prayer. That is the manifested presence of God.

There are other times when God's presence manifests in unusual or unexpected ways. We all have times like this. I remember experiencing just such a time after I lost my grandmother. I was at the hospital when she passed away, and I went into the bathroom and began to cry. I was grieving because I loved my grandmother very much; she had lived with us when I was growing up. As I knelt by the toilet in that little hospital bathroom and cried, all of a sudden it seemed like that little room was filled with the presence of God. I felt as if Jesus were standing there with me, putting His hand on my shoulder. I sensed His presence in such a powerful, tangible way! As I think back on that incident, I am reminded of how wonderful it is to experience the manifested presence of God.

Have you ever met someone who obviously has the presence of God on them? You can't help but notice it. Joseph was a person like that. Even Potiphar noticed it.

Here is my heart's desire: I want to be like that. I want to live in God's manifested presence every moment of every day.

And I hope that you share my desire. If you do, remember that the key to having His presence in your life is obedience.

In the same way that obedience will cause God's presence to manifest in your life, disobedience will cause His presence to leave. We can see a sad example of this occurring in the life of Cain. "Then Cain went out from the presence of the Lord" (Gen. 4:16).

Cain "went out from the presence of the Lord" because he was disobedient. Cain had first disobeyed God in the matter of his offerings, and then Cain had killed his brother Abel. But God gave him a chance to confess what he had done. God asked Cain, "Where is your brother?" Of course, God knew where his brother was. He didn't need Cain to let him know that. He was simply giving Cain an opportunity to confess his sin and repent of it. God was not looking for sinless perfection in Cain—but He was looking for a repentant heart.

But instead of confessing his sin, Cain replied, "Am I my brother's keeper?"—denying any responsibility for what he had done. So God said, "Your brother's blood is crying out to me from the ground." In this way God was telling Cain, "I knew what you did all along. I just wanted you to confess it and acknowledge it as wrong." But Cain refused to confess it and repent; and the result was that Cain "went out from the presence of the Lord." Because of disobedience, the presence of God was no longer manifested in Cain's life.

Disobedience cost Adam and Eve the presence of God as well. They had enjoyed the manifested presence of God in the Garden of Eden. The Bible says that God walked in the garden in the cool of the day. But after Adam and Eve sinned, they hid themselves from God's presence. God came to Adam and gave him a chance to repent and God came to Eve and gave her a chance to repent. But sin caused them to hide from the presence of God.

King David understood the manifested presence of God. He knew what it was to have God's presence rest upon him, and he knew what it was to lose God's presence through disobedience. But David also knew that he could cry out to God in repentance for his sin, asking God to forgive him. In Psalm 51:11 David pleads: "Do not cast me away from Your presence, and do not take Your Holy Spirit from me."

David had disobeyed God, and as a result he had lost God's presence for a time. But when David repented from his heart, the Lord forgave him. When David returned to walking in God's ways, to walking in obedience, the presence of God was restored to David's life.

The presence of God is what makes you prosper in all you do. And obedience is the key to a life that is marked by the presence of God. This presents another question.

What is the key to obedience?

The Key to Obedience: Faith

Some people have actually said, "I know that obedience is important, but I just can't seem to obey God in this certain area. I've tried and tried." You must understand that working out of your own strength—trying hard—is not the answer. The key to a life of obedience is really just faith. Because if you truly *believe* that a life of obedience will produce the blessings of God, you won't *try* to obey Him—you'll *want* to!

Think about it. If you really believe the consequences of a certain action are going to be bad for you, you will decide not to do it. And if you really believe that God is going to reward you for doing the right thing, then you will decide to do that. The critical phrase here is "if you believe," because faith is what produces obedience in our lives.

If you truly believe in something, you will do it. And if you believe what God has said, you will do what He tells you to do. The key to obedience is faith.

Faith is the reason a farmer plants crops. A farmer works and sweats and tills the ground because he *believes* a crop will grow from the seed that he has planted. Faith is not as mysterious as we make it out to be.

Think about it—every day you place your faith in myriad inanimate objects all the time. When you get in your car and turn your key in the ignition, you have faith that it is going to start (rather than burst into flames, jump into the air or start singing "Feelings"). When you turn on the hot water faucet and the water feels cold, you don't conclude that hot water heaters don't work. You just wait—because you believe that eventually it is going to get hot.

But many Christians turn on the faucet of prayer, and if it feels cold at the start, they just turn it off. They have more faith in a hot water heater than they do in God. But when you turn the faucet of prayer on, and leave that faucet on, it is going to get hotter than you could imagine! That is what faith is—believing, even when the water is cold! It is leaving that faucet on, no matter what the circumstances say—because God has said that the hot water is coming, and you believe Him!

If we believe, we will obey. And if we obey, we will eat the "good of the land" (Isa. 1:19). In other words, faith ultimately brings prosperity and the presence of God. So let's keep in mind these words from Exodus: "Now therefore, if you will indeed obey My voice and keep My covenant, then you shall be a special treasure to Me above all people; for all the earth is Mine" (Exod. 19:5). And if we *believe* that, we will want to obey Him. We will want to be a special treasure to our Father God.

Even children have a promise from God regarding obedience.

Children, obey your parents in the Lord, for this is right. "Honor your father and mother," which is the first commandment with promise: "that it may be well with you and you may live long on the earth" (Eph. 6:1-3).

God says that if children honor their parents, they will live long on the earth—and what is even better, God says that it will be well with them (see v. 3). In other words, obedience to parents will bring the blessing of God.

By the way, if things seem as if they have never gone well for you in your life, you may want to ask yourself whether you have failed to honor your parents, because the Bible tells us this is "the first commandment with a promise" (v. 2). In other words, this is a good place to start applying the truths of obedience and blessings. This command does not say to honor your father and your mother if they are good people. It does not say to honor your father and mother if they are Christians. It simply says to honor your father and mother so that things "may be well with you" (v. 3).

I believe one of the reasons that God's favor is on my life is because I've made that commitment to honor my parents. They are not perfect—no one is; but they are my parents. I'm not going to speak negatively about them. I'm going to honor them, as God says that I should. And if I honor them, things will go well with me.

How do children honor their parents? First and foremost by obeying them: "Children, obey your parents in the Lord, for this is right" (Eph. 6:1). Do you know why children obey? Children obey because they believe that things will go well with them if they do. If a child believes that he or she will get a reward by obeying, that belief will definitely influence his or her behavior. And if a child believes that he or she will get a spanking for disobeying, that expectation will influence his or her behavior as well.

When our children were growing up, we rewarded good behavior and we disciplined for bad behavior through spankings. Our children believed that if they did right, I would reward them. And they also believed that if they disobeyed, they would get in trouble. Of course, I would much rather have rewarded them than spanked them—and I'm sure our heavenly Father feels the same way. I loved to reward them with special gifts, because I wanted them to understand that if you do a good thing, God will reward you. I wanted them to learn that obedience truly does result in blessings.

Some children disobey because they don't believe. They don't believe that disobedience will cause anything to not "be well with" them. But it is amazing how quickly that lack of faith can be corrected by a good, old-fashioned spanking! I realize that books have been written that contradict what the Bible has to say about disciplining children. We even have some friends who decided to follow the advice in one of those books, informing us that spanking was no longer necessary in their household. But six months later they let us know that spanking had been reinstated—because discipline doesn't work any other way.

Remember, the key to obedience is faith, or believing. And a spanking helps a child *believe* that obedience brings good results—and that disobedience also brings painful ones!

We adults are not much different from children: We disobey God because we don't *believe* we're really going to suffer any consequences for that disobedience. And if we really *believed* that God rewards us when we obey Him, we would want to obey. The key to obedience is faith.

God swore that those who did not obey Him would not enter His rest. In other words, they would not enter that place in their destiny in which God would bless every aspect of their lives. "And to whom did He swear that they would not enter His rest, but to those who did not obey? So we see that they could not enter in because of unbelief" (Heb. 3:18-19).

And we often assume that they did not enter into their destiny because they did not walk in obedience. But if we read that last verse, we see that it was not really disobedience that prevented them from entering in—it was unbelief. If they had *believed* God's Words, they would have obeyed Him. And if they had obeyed Him, they would have entered into His rest.

God wants every one of us to enter our promised land. Our promised land is a place where the blessing of God is on us, prospering us in everything we do. The key to having that blessing is to have His presence manifested in our lives. The key to His manifested presence is obedience to His commands. And in order to walk in obedience to His commands, we are going to have to believe. We are going to have to have faith.

So what is the key to having faith?

The Key to Faith: Hearing the Word

The key to our having faith is in hearing the Word of God. I want to emphasize this: The key to having faith is not in obeying the Word of God—the key to having faith is in *hearing* the Word of God. Now I believe in obeying the Word, and we must obey God if we want to have His blessing on our lives. But it is not obedience that produces faith. Rather, it is faith that produces obedience. And faith only comes by the Word of God.

This is not my idea. God made this very plain in Romans 10:17 when He said, "So then faith comes by hearing, and hearing by the word of God." This Scripture passage says that if I hear the Word of God, "faith comes." In other words, faith shows up. So all I have to do is hear the Word of God. So there is something about *hearing* the Word of God that produces faith.

Now I know the Bible says that I must be a doer of the Word as well. James 1:22 says, "But be doers of the word, and not hearers only, deceiving yourselves." But it is *hearing* the Word that is the key to doing it! Because the more I hear the Word of God, the more faith I will have. And the more faith I have, the more I will want to obey God and live out the Word.

The reason that a lot of people are not doers of the Word is because they don't really have faith. But the reason they don't have faith is that they haven't heard much of the Word. The Bible says the way that faith comes to us is by *hearing the Word of God*.

So the more of the Word of God that you have in you, the more faith you will have. The more faith you have, the more you will obey. The more you obey, the more the presence of God will manifest in your life. And the more often you live in the presence of God, the more you will prosper and succeed.

Every one of us can prosper, and every one of us can be successful! And the way we begin is by hearing the Word of God. So start to make the Word of God part of your life. Listen to His Word whenever you can. Read the Bible daily. Memorize Scripture passages, meditate on them, and write verses on note cards to tape on your mirror. If you hear His Word consistently, faith will naturally come. God promised that it would. And as your faith increases, you will find that you are walking in obedience. As you walk in obedience, you're going to have the presence of God on your life. And if the presence of God is with you, you're going to succeed!

There are no words to describe the blessing of having God's presence in your life. Right now I can feel that the favor of God is on my life, and it is a wonderful thing. It is so wonderful that I don't want to do one single thing to mess it up! The favor of God makes you feel that nothing is impossible. The favor of God makes you feel that anything you attempt to do for God will succeed. Because when you sense that God is with you, you know your efforts on His behalf will not fail.

What could possibly be worth losing that blessing, that favor, that manifested presence of God? I don't want to walk in disobedience, because I know that if I disobey God, His presence will leave my life. And I don't want to lose His presence or His favor!

So it really wasn't a hard thing that day at the airport to leave a note on the car I had bumped. It really wasn't hard to decide that we would miss our plane. It was easy to do the right thing—*when I remembered that God has called me to be faithful in small matters, as well as great, as I live out my destiny according to His will.*

I want to walk in the destiny God has planned for me. And I know that if I am to be set over much, I must be found faithful in little things— even a crack in a piece of plastic on an old car.

Eventually I received a call from the lady whose vehicle had been damaged. I apologized for the accident and gave her our insurance information so that she could get her bumper repaired. But before we got off the phone, she said, "I just have to ask you a question. I have shown your note to everyone in my office, and no one can believe that you actually left a note. It would have been so easy to just drive away. We don't know if you're a saint, a space alien or what—but none of us can figure out why you would leave a note."

This woman was an unbeliever. Yet, like Potiphar, she recognized that there was something different about my behavior. So I was able to explain to her the reason that I had left that note. I was able to share the gospel with her and tell her how Jesus Christ had changed my life—and that He could change her life also. "You said that everyone in your office wants to know why I left that note," I said to her. "Be sure that you tell them. Be sure to tell them that the reason I left that note is because Jesus Christ has changed my life—and He wants to do that for all of them, too."

There is nothing on this earth that can compare to the joy of a moment like that. A moment when the presence of God rests upon you, a moment when you are able to do something very important for Him. But it all begins by being faithful in the smallest things—by being a faithful steward. If I had not been faithful to do the right thing about that accident, I would never have had the opportunity to be God's messenger to the people in that office. And I would have risked losing the presence of God in my life—a blessing which is shared only with those who walk closely with Him in obedience.

So, remember that faithfulness—good stewardship—is what causes us to be successful in everything we do. It is what caused Joseph to be successful. It is what causes us to have the favor of God and His presence in our lives. And I want all of us to have God's favor on our lives. The wonderful truth is that God's favor is available to everyone and anyone!

You can live in the favor, the blessing and the prosperity of God. God can bless you and He wants to bless you.

So be faithful in little things. Be a good employee, a good steward "as to the Lord" (Col. 3:23). Spend time in God's Word and watch your faith increase. As faith comes, obedience will naturally follow. And when you honor God and walk in obedience to Him, He will honor you with His presence. Then His favor and blessings will rest on your life, and, like Joseph, you will prosper in all that you do.

And then you will know that you've passed the test of stewardship. You can look forward with joy to hearing Him say, "Well done, good and faithful servant; you were faithful over a few things, I will make you ruler over many things. Enter into the joy of your lord" (Matt. 25:21).

CHAPTER FOUR

THE PURITY TEST

It had been unusually quiet as I preached that Sunday.

Now, I don't pastor the most vocal congregation in the world. Nevertheless, on most occasions I can count on a steady scattering of "amens," and "that's rights." But not this day. Throughout my sermon, though my preaching was often passionate, the crowd remained somber and silent.

My topic? Sexual purity.

Afterward, I was asked an interesting question: "Why do you suppose there weren't very many 'Amens' today?"

"What do you think?" was my only reply.

It is actually rather odd that the subject of sexuality would make any of us uncomfortable these days. After all, we live in a society that appears to be absolutely saturated with sex and sensuality. And it seems bent on making us as comfortable as can be about sex and related matters!

In the recent past, our country endured a scandal involving immorality at the highest level of elected office. Some were genuinely appalled; others merely viewed the incident from a political standpoint. The majority, however, couldn't care less. But what shocked me most about this very sad chapter in our history was the widely held idea that the President's private behavior had nothing to do with his leadership of our country. Nothing could be further from the truth.

Whatever your political views, you must understand that there are certain truths that will never change—and God has spelled out these truths quite clearly for us in the Bible.

The Purity Test: Sexual Stewardship

Our popular culture may declare that sexual morality has nothing to do with character; but God begs to differ: Sexual morality has *everything* to do with character. And character is very important to God. So if we want to walk in the destinies that God has planned, we are going to have to understand what He has to say about sexual purity.

Don't misunderstand what I'm saying here—God made us to be sexual beings. He wants every person to enjoy a wonderful, fulfilling sex life with his or her spouse. But just as with every other gift God has given us, we have a responsibility to steward that gift in a way that is pleasing to Him. God is watching to see if we will be faithful stewards in this area of our lives as well. Remember, if we are faithful in little things, God knows that He can trust us with much. But if we are unfaithful in little things, God says that we will also be unfaithful in much (see Luke 16:10).

It is very important to understand this—because a person who will be immoral in this area of his or her life will also be immoral in other areas. A person who will cheat on his or her spouse will also cheat his or her employer (or his or her country). This is not an idea that I came up with. This is simply *what God has said in His Word*. God said that someone who will be unfaithful in a small thing will also be unfaithful in a large thing (see Luke 16:10). I didn't say that—Jesus did! So our sexual conduct does matter very much to God. It is very important that we be found faithful in this area of our lives.

Character is a foundational issue. If character goes, the rest of the house goes. If the foundation is bad, everything else will be bad. We can never "just" be sexually immoral—because sexual immorality opens the door to a host of other sins. If we are sexually immoral, we will also lie and be deceptive, because we have to cover up our sin. The Bible says that King David was "a man after [God's] own heart" (Acts 13:22). Yet sexual immorality drove him to lie, and eventually even to murder, in an attempt to cover up his sin.

That's why I'm so saddened to see our culture has declined to the point that many would say a leader's sexual immorality has no bearing on his leadership ability. Appalling as this is, it is a sobering indication that our nation needs revival and repentance—and it ought to stir us to search our own hearts and to pray. But whatever ideas the popular culture may be promoting, only God's ideas really matter.

In God's kingdom, character has everything to do with fitness for leadership. God says that we must be found faithful in small things before He will set us over much (see Luke 16:10). So it is important for us to understand that if we allow any compromise in this area, we are putting our God-given destiny at risk.

Of course, God is a redeemer by nature. If we have fallen in this area and we sincerely repent from our hearts before God, He will forgive and restore us. But if we persist in immorality, we will not step into our destiny. Why? Because God is looking for faithful stewards whom He can trust wholeheartedly.

This is the Purity Test—and in our sensual society each one of us faces this critical test on a daily basis. But we can all draw inspiration from the story of Joseph. When faced with great temptation, Joseph passed this test with flying colors! Genesis 39 tells the story.

> And it came to pass after these things that his master's wife cast longing eyes on Joseph, and she said, "Lie with me." But he refused and said to his master's wife, "Look, my master does not know what is with me in the house, and he has committed all that he has to my hand. There is no one greater in this house than I, nor has he kept back anything from me but you, because you are his wife. How then can I do this great wickedness, and sin against God?" So it was, as she spoke to Joseph day by day, that he did not heed her, to lie with her or to be with her. But it happened about this time, when Joseph went into the house to do his work, and none of the men of the house was inside, that she caught him by his garment, saying, "Lie with me." But he left his

garment in her hand, and fled and ran outside (Gen. 39:7-12).

One reason Joseph passed this test with flying colors is very simple: When the temptation became too great for him to walk away—he ran! God advises us to follow Joseph's example and to "flee sexual immorality" (1 Cor. 6:18). The literal meaning of that word "flee" is "to run away."[1] So God doesn't say that we should just walk away from immorality. He tells us to run from it! And that is exactly what Joseph did—even though he had to leave his garment in Potiphar's wife's hand in order to get away.

Notice what Joseph calls immorality—"great wickedness, and sin against God" (Gen. 39:9). Joseph ran away from temptation because he understood something that our society seems to have forgotten—that sexual immorality is evil and sinful. And Joseph knew that the wrong done would not only be against his master Potiphar. Joseph also understood that sexual immorality would be a wrong done against God—that it would harm his relationship with his Lord. So Joseph ran.

In many ways this is just another aspect of the test of faithful stewardship, because in the Ten Commandments, God forbids us to covet anything that belongs to our neighbor, including our neighbor's wife (see Exod. 20:17). Potiphar's wife was deliberately tempting Joseph to covet her, so Joseph's stewardship was now being tested in that area. The question was no longer whether Joseph could steward another man's *things* faithfully. Rather, now it was, Could he exercise faithful stewardship of another man's *wife*?

But there is an even more important question here. Could Joseph steward his own body? Could he steward his own appetites and desires? Would Joseph serve God faithfully in that area of his life?

This is a very important question and one that each of us will have to face. We like to think we can discipline ourselves to walk with God, to spend time in the Word and to spend time in prayer. But many of us cannot even steward our physical appetites in a way that is honoring to God. This is one of the first areas in which we must learn to discipline ourselves, because if we cannot bring our own bodies under control, how will we be faithful in any other area? The apostle Paul understood this.

In 1 Corinthians 9:27, he said, "I discipline my body and bring it into subjection, lest, when I have preached to others, I myself should become disqualified."

If we don't want to be disqualified from our God-given destiny, we must learn to keep our physical body under control—and not only in the area of food. We must bring our sexual appetite under control as well.

Sexual temptation is an issue every person must confront. I was once speaking at a men's retreat and I asked the question, "How many of you men have ever struggled with lust?" Around 90 percent of the men raised their hands. So I reflected a bit and then said, "Well, it's obvious the other 10 percent of you struggle with lying!"

Dealing with sexual temptation is simply a part of who we are—because God created us to be sexual beings.

Let's get real. Dealing with sexual temptation is simply a part of who we are—because God has created us to be sexual beings. He made us as sexual creatures, and He wants us to enjoy that aspect of our identity. As with everything else God has created, He has a wonderful plan for that part of our lives. But are we going to follow His plan, as laid out in His Word—or are we going to walk in disobedience?

Remember, the path of obedience is always the path of God's blessing. The path of obedience is always the path of God's promotion. So if we want to fulfill His dream for our lives, we are going to have to bring this area under God's control.

I believe God has shown me some keys that will help you understand how to pass this important test.

Impurity Begins in the Eye, Not in the Heart

Since lust is in the mind (or heart), it might be easy to assume that impurity begins in that area. But it doesn't. Impurity actually begins in the eye. It begins with looking.

Notice that the Scripture passage says Potiphar's wife "cast longing eyes on Joseph" (Gen. 39:7). The Bible tells us that Joseph was a handsome man (see v. 6), so I suppose it is only natural that she would notice that he was attractive. But at some point she began to not only notice Joseph, but also to "look" at him. After she started looking at Joseph, it was only a matter of time before looking turned into longing—or lust, to put it bluntly. When "noticing" turned into looking, that was when lust was stirred up. So the impurity began in her eyes, when she started to look at Joseph longingly.

Here is some advice that will go a long way toward steering clear of immorality: Don't *look* at handsome or beautiful people! Don't allow yourself to look or to continue looking—because if you allow yourself to continue to look, you are inviting lust into your life. Look away.

David's sin of adultery began when he wandered out onto the roof and happened to see Bathsheba bathing (see 2 Sam. 11:2)—but how long did he look? Instead of looking, David could have turned and looked the other way. He could have walked back into his house and cried out to the Lord for help. But instead he continued to look—and lust was inevitably stirred up.

When I was a teenager, my youth pastor was trying to help us in this area, and he told us, "The second look is lust." Unfortunately, that advice didn't seem to help me very much—because I just took one very long first look!

When you think about it, Joseph probably had lots of opportunities to look, if he had wanted to. Joseph was the steward of the house, and he had charge of everything in it. He probably knew when his master's wife bathed and when she dressed—and she was most likely a beautiful woman. It wouldn't have been difficult for Joseph to look when the occasion arose. But if Joseph had allowed himself to look, he would have given lust an opportunity to invade his heart—and he probably would have fallen into sin when the temptation came.

The reason Joseph didn't fall when temptation came was because lust was not in his heart. And lust was not in his heart because he had not allowed it into his eyes.

"Don't look" should become a motto for all of us. Don't look at pornography. Don't look at inappropriate sites on the Internet. Don't look at movies that are sexually explicit. Don't look at television programs that are seductive. Men, if you see a woman who is not dressed appropriately, the first thought that should come to your mind ought to be, *Don't look!*—because if you look, lust is the next step. And after lust is immorality.

This is a practical thing that all of us can do. So let's remember to control our looking!

We've all heard this convenient lie: "I'll just look, but I won't do anything." You know how well that works. Have you ever heard someone say, "I'm just going to look; I'm not going to buy"? It doesn't work. If you look, you will buy because looking gets your desire stirred up. If you start looking for homes, you're going to buy a new house. If you start looking for cars, you *will* buy a new car—the auto dealers call it new-car fever.

We bought a new home a while back, and for some reason I started looking at these new stainless steel barbecue grills. They are so bright and shiny, and I guess guys just like shiny things. Of course, I already had a perfectly good barbecue grill. It worked just fine, but it was black. It wasn't shiny like those new ones. Somehow I started looking at the new ones, and every time we went into a store, I'd say to Debbie, "I'm going to go look at the barbecue grills."

But I got to thinking and praying about it, as I pray over every financial decision. And I felt like the Lord said to me, "You don't need a new barbecue grill. Stop looking!" If I had continued looking, I would have eventually bought one. So what I had to do was to just stop looking.

Here is my point: If you're not going to buy a barbecue grill, don't go to the store where they are sold.

And if you're not in the market for adultery, don't lust after beautiful people. Don't drive by that adult bookstore. Don't wander into the adult section at the video store. Don't pick up that sensual magazine. Don't look!

Let me show you what a thoroughly biblical principle this is. Psalm 101:3 says, "I will set nothing wicked before my eyes."

What if we purposed to do that—to set nothing wicked before our eyes? Think about how that would affect us, just in terms of the movies and TV programs we watch. Every time we go to a movie or pick up a magazine, we are setting something before our eyes, so we should be careful about the movies we watch and the magazines we read. And we should resolve to set before our eyes nothing that could stir up temptation.

Proverbs 27:20 says, "Hell and Destruction are never full; so the eyes of man are never satisfied." The Bible says the *eyes* are never satisfied. So the eyes have a lust of their own. This is also described in 1 John 2:16 as "the lust of the flesh, the lust of the eyes, and the pride of life." So there is lust of the eyes, or to put it another way, a lust of looking.

In Matthew 5:28 Jesus tells us, "But I say to you that whoever looks at a woman to lust for her has already committed adultery with her in his heart. And if your right eye causes you to sin, pluck it out and cast it from you." Jesus is showing us a progression here. He is telling us that the *eye* can cause us to sin. He is talking about the sin of looking. The progression He describes involves first looking, then lusting and finally immorality. Before immorality occurs, there is lust. But before lust is stirred up, there is looking. So, implicitly, He's giving us some real wisdom here: Stop looking!

Jesus tells us more about the eyes in Matthew 6:22-23: "The lamp of the body is the eye. If therefore your eye is good, your whole body will be full of light. But if your eye is bad, your whole body will be full of darkness." Jesus is saying that what we set before our eyes is what will eventually end up in our hearts and will affect our entire body. If we continue to set darkness before our eyes, our bodies will end up full of that darkness. If we look at things that stir up lust, our bodies will end up full of that lust. So we must set before our eyes what is good and wholesome. If we set what is "light" before our eyes, our entire being will be affected by that light.

Job said, "I have made a covenant with my eyes; why then should I look upon a young woman?" (Job 31:1). That is a good Scripture passage for every man to memorize! Job made a covenant with his eyes, and you should do it too. Make a covenant with your eyes, and make a covenant with God at the same time. Say to God, "I will not look! If I see something I know is seductive, I will look away. I will not look a second time. I will not look a long time. I will look away."

I know only too well that the eyes can open the door to darkness, because the Lord has really dealt with me in this area of my life. For many years this was a very difficult area of struggle for me.

The Importance of Honesty
One thing you need to understand is that Satan works in the darkness. So if you have a difficulty in this area, you need to expose it and uncover it. Because the more you keep it hidden, the more power you give to Satan.

A man who struggles with lust is often afraid to come clean with his wife about this, because he is afraid that she will reject him. He needs to understand that it is actually his deception that destroys his wife's trust, not the lust. It is the lying and covering up that could cause his wife to reject him or lose respect for him.

I have talked to many couples that have suffered in this area of their marriage. In every case, it was the deception and resulting loss of trust that hurt the spouse the most, far more deeply than the immorality.

The Importance of Accountability
So if you struggle in this area, run to your spouse, not away from him or her. Go to your spouse and say, "I love you. I want only you. But sexual temptation is so pervasive in our society, and I've adopted some practices that I should not have. I don't want to do these things anymore, and I want to make myself accountable." It will help you immeasurably

if you will just be honest, be open about it and make yourself account-able to someone.

Years ago I made the decision to be accountable, not only to Debbie but also to my friends. Being accountable has not been easy, but it has proved to be a good and healthy thing.

Just a few months ago one of the elders of our church checked up on me, and that didn't offend me at all.

He asked me, "How are you doing in this area?"

I said, "I'm doing very well in this area. Thank you for asking. Debbie and I are doing great, and I'm doing well."

"Great," he said. "I know that God is blessing us as a church. And I just want you to know that I'll help you, if this area should become a problem. If the enemy attacks you, I want you to know that you've got a brother who will help you."

I appreciated that. That is a good thing! That is healthy!

But arriving at the decision to be accountable is not always easy or comfortable. When I decided to make myself accountable to Debbie, we had been married about seven years. I sat her down and said to her, "I need to come clean with you about my past. You know that I have an immoral past—but I want to tell you *everything* about my past." Then I told her everything.

Now I have a very bad past, and I thought she would be shocked. I was actually afraid she would leave me. I was afraid she would say, "You're a pervert"—and then leave. That is really what I thought. But despite my fears, I knew that I needed to bring my struggle out into the open. So I said to her, "That's it, there is the truth. That is who you real-ly married."

But God had a surprise for me. Instead of rejecting me, Debbie said, "I knew that you were bad when I married you. I knew that, but I love you anyway. One thing I really love about you is that you're not dishon-est about it. You know when you've been bad, you tell God when you've been bad, and you allow God to work in your life. That is the best thing that you can do."

Then I told her that I had a habit I needed to break—a habit of look-ing. And I asked for her help. I made myself accountable to her.

"I don't want to look, but I need some help," I said. "Will you help me? If you see me looking, I want you to pray for me. I want you to talk to me about it. And I want you to call me on it."

I had no idea how quickly my request would be answered. Soon after that we took a vacation and were at the swimming pool. Needless to say, that is a very hard place not to look! Sure enough, a lady walked by me and I was looking. The next thing I knew, Debbie had reached over and pinched me right where no person should ever be pinched—on the back of my arm. She grabbed my skin in a very painful squeeze, looked into my eyes with intense determination and asked with great seriousness in her voice, "Do I need to pray for you?"

Don't let anyone deceive you. Immorality in your own life will have a negative impact on the lives of your children.

Believe me, after several pinches like that, you quit looking! If you have struggled with looking and with lust, I want to encourage you to become accountable to someone whom you trust. It has helped me, and it will help you too. Bringing your struggles into the light is a good and healthy thing. Because lust does not begin in the heart—it begins in the eyes.

Impurity Will Affect Your Family

If someone tells you that impurity will not affect your children, that person is either a liar or is greatly deceived. Your children *will* be affected if you allow impurity to become part of your life.

In 2 Samuel 11, we find an illustration of this reality. This passage describes how David fell into adultery with Bathsheba. And by chapter 13, we are reading about how his children began to commit gross immorality. Isn't that amazing?

I believe David had a chance to stop the sin in his children, but he didn't see it coming. And the reason he didn't see it coming was because that weakness was in his own life. He had a blind spot for that weakness in his kids, because he had the same weakness. So don't let anyone deceive you. Immorality in your own life will have a negative impact on the lives of your children.

The Bible says the iniquity of the fathers is passed down to the children.

God . . . keeping mercy for thousands, forgiving iniquity and transgression and sin, by no means clearing the guilty, visiting the iniquity of the fathers upon the children and the children's children to the third and the fourth generation (Exod. 34:6-7).

So if we do not deal with the iniquity in our own lives, we will see it repeated in the lives of our children. That is simply what the Bible says. But notice that this passage does not say that the *sins* of the fathers are passed down to the children (even though it is frequently quoted this way). Rather, it speaks of the *iniquity* that is passed down.

Lust is an iniquity. And iniquity dwells in the heart.

There is an important difference between sin and iniquity. Sin is the outward movement, and iniquity is the inward motivation. Sin is the action, and iniquity is the attitude. Sin is in the hand, and iniquity is in the heart.

If iniquity is in the heart, the hand will follow accordingly. If the attitude is in the heart, then the action will follow. Therefore, if we want to overcome our struggles in the area of sexual purity, we must deal with the inward motivation. We have to deal with the iniquity because the iniquities, or the hidden things of the heart, are what our children will inherit from us.

The word "sin" means to "trespass," to transgress or to step over the line.[2] If you step onto another person's property, and a Private Property sign is posted, you are trespassing. That is transgression, and that is what sin is. Sin is going where you are not supposed to go or stepping over the line that you are not supposed to cross.

When God says, "Don't step over this line," and we step over it—that is sin. That is transgression. But the heart attitude behind that action is iniquity. For example, adultery is sin; but lust is iniquity. Adultery is the outward movement, but lust is the inward motivation. We need to understand that lust is an iniquity, and iniquity is in the heart.

I've heard some men say, "Well, I know I deal with this stuff, but I've never actually transgressed. I've never put that lust into action. Sure, I look at pornography and have a difficulty with lust. But I've always been faithful to my wife."

Such a person needs to understand that it is not the *sins* of the parents which are passed down to the children; it is the *iniquities*. If we allow lust to stay in our hearts, we are going to see it in our children; because God said He would visit the *iniquities* of the fathers on the children to the third and fourth generation (see Exod. 20:5).

Here's the great news. God has made a way for us to be free from both our sins and our iniquities. Isaiah 53:5 says, "But He was wounded for our transgressions, He was bruised for our iniquities." (Remember, *transgressions* are outward and relate to our sins or trespasses. *Iniquities* are inward and have to do with our heart.) Jesus was wounded outwardly for our outward transgressions and sins. And He was also bruised inwardly for our inward iniquities.

In other words, everything that needs to be done for us to be set free from sin and iniquity has been done in Jesus Christ through His extraordinary sacrifice. Jesus has set us free from sin and iniquity by His atoning work on the Cross. But if we don't allow Him to set us free in the area of iniquity, we will give our children an inheritance we don't want them to have.

Impurity Is Always Lust, Not Love

To young people, I would say, "If you're dating someone and they say, 'If you love me, you'll do it,' that is a lie." Impurity is always lust, never love!

If you are in an adulterous relationship, it is not love; it is lust. Potiphar's wife did not love Joseph—she lusted after him. If she loved him, she would not have lied about him and allowed him to sit in a prison for 10 years.

Most sin is born of selfishness, and lust is the most selfish sin there is. Lust does not want gratification for anyone but self. Lust doesn't care whether the spouse gets hurt. Lust doesn't care if the kids get hurt. If you allow it, lust will take over. And it will affect not only you, but your family as well. You need to know that.

Sexual immorality has consequences (and they are not the consequences that love produces). Those consequences bring great pain and heartache, and we need to make sure our children understand that. Sometimes we don't adequately explain to them why God says, "Don't step over that line." God is not a prude who does not want you to have fun. God warns you to not step over that line because He knows that pain and death are on the other side. He loves you, and He doesn't want you to take that road to destruction!

I was once asked by a young couple, "If we love each other, and we're going to get married anyway, what difference does a piece of paper make?"

"None," was my reply. "The piece of paper [marriage license] makes no difference at all. I'll tell you what does make a difference, though—the blessing of God. It makes all the difference in the world!"

Who would not want the blessing of God on their sexual relationship with their spouse? When we walk in obedience to God, we will have His blessing. But if we walk in disobedience to God, we have invited destruction into that area of our lives—and the only way to close that door is through repentance.

Young people are under tremendous pressure from the world to compromise, and they need to understand these truths. But some couples who have been married for years also need to understand this—because they may have opened this door and don't know how to shut it. Well, if that last statement describes you, please keep reading—I can help you shut that door!

I have observed that premarital sex can open the door to dissatisfaction with sex after the wedding vows have been spoken. Because if you are going to have premarital sex, you will have to sneak around to do it.

All impurity involves deception. So if you had premarital sex, you had to do some sneaking around. And that developed an appetite for "sneaking around sex"—an appetite God never intended you to develop. By compromising in this way, you set your marriage up for failure.

I know that may seem like a strong statement, but I have witnessed the sad results of this all too often. When I counsel couples that have gone through adultery, I have learned to ask them about this: "I'm not trying to pry, but I need to know, so we can shut a door. Did the two of you have premarital sex?" In nearly every case they say, "Yes."

Here is how it happens. When you have premarital sex, you sneak around and get butterflies in your stomach. You get that adrenaline rush because you're doing something that is forbidden and exciting. But after you get married, you don't have to sneak around anymore, and that adrenaline rush is gone. Then the man will start to say, "It's just not the same," and he'll want to begin to do other things—X-rated videos, pornography and other things like that—because he is trying to satisfy an appetite that was created by sin.

That is why a man will begin to talk to the secretary at his office and begin to flirt with her—he's trying to satisfy an appetite for the forbidden that was aroused in him by premarital sex. And then he will begin to engage in an extramarital affair with her. In order to do that, what will he have to do? That's right—sneak around. He'll get the same adrenaline rush with her that he had with his wife before they got married. He associates that feeling with love, so he'll begin to think he loves her and not his wife. So he'll divorce his wife and marry her.

Think about it. Now what happens? He doesn't have to sneak around anymore—and now the cycle of sin and deception is ready to repeat itself. That is why some people have been divorced three, four and five times. They are trying to satisfy an appetite God never intended us to have—an appetite that was created by lust, not love.

If you want to close the door that premarital sex has created, you do so the same way you close it with any other sin—go to God and repent. Unfortunately, many Christian couples that have had premarital sex don't want to admit it. They want to just gloss it over, pretending to others and to themselves that it never happened. But it did happen, and until that sin is repented of, it will continue to affect them.

If that is you, I am not trying to condemn you, and I am not saying that you have to broadcast your failings to the world. But if you want to shut that door, you cannot just gloss over the fact that you had pre-marital sex. You have to deal with it as sin. You have to go to your spouse and ask forgiveness for having violated God's commandments. You're going to have to call sin "sin" and repent to one another and to God. The two of you are going to have to pray for each other and pray for forgiveness. Because if you don't deal with it as sin, you will leave an open door for the enemy into your marriage. It is very important that you close that door. If you don't, it will affect your marriage, your family and your children.

Impurity Will Affect Your Relationship with God

Your family relationships are not the only ones affected by immorality. Immorality will negatively impact your relationship with God, as well. Why? Because immorality brings with it great deception—and God is a God of Truth. There is no falseness, or deception, in Him.

Immorality always involves deception, because in order to be involved in sin, you will have to sneak around. Any person who is involved in immorality is a deceptive liar—that is the bottom line. Now I realize that is a strong statement, but I am not looking down on anyone. I am simply describing the way I used to be! I know what I am talking about, because I used to be a very immoral person. (In other words, I speak from experience!)

Immoral people cover up, they lie, and they become deceptive in every area of their lives. And by doing that, they eventually learn to be deceptive not only with their spouse or their parents—they also learn how to be deceptive with God.

Please don't misunderstand me—God cannot be deceived! He knows exactly what you and I are doing. But when you open your life to impurity, you open yourself to demonic spirits. And those spirits will tell you that no one sees what you are doing—not even God.

You can't be involved in impurity and also have an open and transparent relationship with God. You may go to church and raise your hands, but you cover your heart. You learn how to pray without dealing with sin. But what does God say about those kinds of prayers?

Psalm 66:18 says, "If I regard iniquity in my heart, the Lord will not hear [me]." Then Proverbs 28:9 tells us: "One who turns away his ear from hearing the law, even his prayer is an abomination."

Don't be deceived. If you are involved in an immoral relationship, it will stand between you and true fellowship with God. When deception takes over, you can convince yourself that sin doesn't matter, that you can still hear from God. But you are not really hearing from God. You may hear a spirit talking to you—but it is not the Holy Spirit!

Those who are involved in immorality become blinded to the point that they can't even see their sin. And they come to believe

Immorality opens the door to great deception. One couple that was involved in an immoral relationship went so far as to tell me that they prayed together. I am going to admit that those words actually made me feel sick—because that is the height of deception. They may be talking to "a" spirit with such prayers—but the spirit they are talking to is not holy! They start to believe that spirit is God, but it is actually a demonic spirit masquerading as an angel of light. Those who are involved in immorality become blinded to the point that they can't even see their sin. And they come to believe that God does not see it either.

You cannot have an open relationship with God if you're walking in impurity. If you persist in immorality, your lying and deception will become a way of life. You will learn how to be a religious person, rather than a godly person. You will learn how to go to church and put a "face" on. You will learn how to go to prayer with a "face" on. And eventually, you will even learn to go to God with a "face" on. But God is not fooled by that "face."

In the end, you will also have learned how to tune out the voice of the Holy Spirit. Because you know the Holy Spirit is saying to you over and over again, "Turn away from that sin. Turn away; turn back to God; turn back to what is right." The reason He is pleading with you is because He sees that the end of that road is death. He sees that the end of that road is destruction—a broken family, a broken marriage and a broken life. He sees that. He loves you. And He is pleading with you to come back.

But if you allow lust to stay in your heart, you will learn how to walk in a rebellious relationship with the Holy Spirit. You will learn how to say no to the Holy Spirit over and over again. You will learn to tune out the voice of God and grieve the Holy Spirit.

Do not be deceived. Immorality will affect your relationship with God. If you believe you can keep immorality in your heart and still have a pure relationship with God, you have been deceived.

This is precisely why James wrote this to the church:

> But each one is tempted when he is drawn away by his own desires and enticed. Then, when desire has conceived, it gives birth to sin; and sin, when it is full-grown, brings forth death. Do not be deceived, my beloved brethren (Jas. 1:14-16).

James is wondering, *How in the world could you go back to your sinful ways now? How could you allow that lust to draw you away from the truth? You must have been deceived—because you know that lust will turn into sin, and that sin will result in death.*

James is pleading with believers not to be deceived but to let God do a work in this area of their lives. And if you are deceived, God is pleading with you also. Because the only way you can have a relationship with God is if you renounce sin and repent. You must come to God on His terms, not yours. You must repent, renounce that sin and tell God that you want to come back to Him.

It is vital. Because if you allow sin to thrive in this area of your life, you will not fulfill your destiny.

Impurity Will Affect Your Future

Satan will try to persuade you that immorality will have no real impact on you, your family or your future. And he can sometimes present a pretty convincing case.

It would be hard to find a case that looked more convincing than Joseph's. After all, Joseph was a slave. He had no rights. He had no future. He could never get married. He could never have a family of his own. Even if he was allowed to marry, his wife would be a slave also—the property of another man. His future held no promise of any kind of sexual fulfillment. So what did he really have to lose by yielding to temptation?

The truth is that Joseph had everything to lose. Because sinning against God would have cost him his fellowship with God. And in losing his communion with God, he would have lost the key to his destiny. He would have lost what God had planned for his future, if he had not passed that test in the "now."

Joseph had everything to lose. And so do you. But that is not what the enemy will tell you in a moment of temptation. Satan will tell you there will be no real consequences to immorality. He will tell you that no one will ever know. I can tell you two people who will *definitely* know: God and you.

Immorality is disobedience toward God. Such disobedience to God will cause His favor and blessing to leave your life. And it will cost you the presence of God that you need in order to reach your destiny.

What Is the Answer?

What is the answer to overcoming the temptations that surround us? How can we pass the test of purity on a continuing basis and be counted faithful to walk in our destiny? We can see the answer by looking once again at the way Joseph passed this test.

The Bible says Potiphar's wife spoke to Joseph "day by day" (Gen. 39:10). So Joseph had to deal with that temptation on a daily basis. Every day she tried to get Joseph to sin. And every day Joseph had to lean on God for strength to resist. Every day Joseph had to trust in God to help him.

Joseph had many opportunities to sin. If lust had been in his heart, eventually he would have fallen. But when the temptation became too great, he finally just ran away. The reason he had the strength to run away is that he had not allowed lust a place in his heart. He had kept lust *out* of his heart by allowing God a place *in* his heart, each and every day. Joseph had learned the secret of walking with God day by day.

Here is the answer to gaining the victory in this area. Just like Joseph, you will encounter temptations on a daily basis. And like Joseph, you must deal with those temptations by trusting in God day by day.

You know, the enemy does not take a day off from attacking you. He will set temptation before you day by day. So you can't take a day off either. You have to rely on God day by day.

Day by day you have to pray.

Day by day you have to fill your mind with the Word of God.

Day by day you must choose not to "look."

Day by day you must trust in God to help you.

The secret to victory in the area of purity is simply *trusting in God every single day.* If you go to God every day and ask for His help, He will strengthen you every day to resist temptation. He will give you the ability every day to walk in purity and obedience to Him.

If you are in bondage in some area, I want to encourage you to turn to God. Don't run away from God—run to Him! He is not condemning you. He is pleading with you to come to Him for help. If you've messed up, go to God. He is your answer! If you just lean on Him day by day, He will be there to help you day by day. And day by day you will start to gain the victory in this area of your life.

It is amazing to me how often people who have fallen in this area are so filled with shame that they don't want to confess it before God.

Guess what—He already knows! And long before you sinned, Jesus Christ had already paid the price to set you free. Satan is the one who doesn't want you to confess your sin. He wants to keep that sin in the dark, so he can continue to have power over you. If you want to be free from sin, the very best thing you can do is confess it. Because when you bring that sin out into the light, you immediately take away Satan's power.

No matter what the enemy may say, disobedience in the area of purity will delay you on the road to your destiny. It is crucial that you bring these matters before God, and allow Him to work in your life.

If you have fallen into sin, I want you to know that there is hope. You can get back on the road to your destiny. Our God is a God of grace and a God of mercy. He gave His only Son to make a way for you to be forgiven and set free. If you repent and turn away from that sin with your whole heart, then He will forgive you, and He can restore you. But it will require deep brokenness and deep repentance on your part. Turn away from sin and turn to God in transparency and humility.

On the other hand, you may not be struggling in this area right now. Perhaps you have learned to trust in God every day, to run away from immorality, to look away from temptation. That is a wonderful thing, and you ought to give praise and thanks to God for His grace and His redeeming power in your life.

Still, I believe there is wisdom for everyone in the words that Paul shares with us: "Therefore let him who thinks he stands take heed lest he fall" (1 Cor. 10:12).

We live in a sensual society, a society that will constantly tempt us to compromise and to sin. Every one of us must "take heed" in order to pass the Purity Test. We must cry out to God to help us be a pure people, a holy people. We must lean on Him every day for the grace to walk in purity before Him. Because our God has commanded us, "You shall be holy, for I the LORD your God am holy" (Lev. 19:2).

And it is only when we are found faithful in the test of purity that His presence and His blessing can rest upon our lives. It is only then that we will be able to walk in the fullness of the destiny that God has planned for each of us.

CHAPTER FIVE

THE PRISON TEST

Joseph passed the purity test with flying colors. In spite of the fact that he was a slave, in spite of the fact that it looked like he had nothing to lose, Joseph chose to do the right thing. When the temptation became too great, he ran away, rather than take the chance that he might yield to sin. He chose to honor God and to honor his responsibility as the steward of his master's household (see Gen. 39:7-12).

Here's a question: Because Joseph had made the decision to walk in obedience, no matter the price, he had every reason to expect to have the blessing of God on his life, right?

Let's look at exactly what happened.

And so it was, when she saw that he had left his garment in her hand and fled outside, that she called to the men of her house and spoke to them, saying, "See, he has brought in to us a Hebrew to mock us. He came in to me to lie with me, and I cried out with a loud voice. And it happened, when he heard that I lifted my voice and cried out, that he left his garment with me, and fled and went outside." So she kept his garment with her until his master came home. Then she spoke to him with words like these, saying, "The Hebrew servant whom you brought to us came in to me to mock me; so it happened, as I lifted my voice and cried out, that he left his garment with me and fled outside." So it was, when his master heard the words which his wife spoke to him, saying, "Your servant did to me after this manner," that his anger was aroused. Then Joseph's master took him and put him into the prison, a place where the king's prisoners were confined. And he was there in the prison (Gen. 39:13-20).

Yes, Joseph chose to do the right thing. But the immediate reward he got for it was to be lied about, falsely accused and thrown into prison! Not exactly the results we would expect to see from such a God-honoring decision. What's wrong with this picture?

The Prison Test: Persevering

Unfortunately, this picture simply reflects what can and does happen in the fallen world in which we live. Make no mistake about it; we must obey God if we want to walk in His blessings. But obedience to God is no guarantee that bad things will never happen to us! Just like Joseph, we must choose to do the right thing if we want to have the presence of God in our lives. But sometimes, just like Joseph, we will do the right thing and get the wrong results. When that happens, we are going through what I call the Prison Test.

The Prison Test could also be called the Perseverance Test, because this is the longest of all the tests. This is a test that lasts for years—and every one of us will go through the Prison Test in some area of our lives. When we do the right thing and end up in the middle of a long and difficult trial, we are going through the Prison Test. It is there that we learn to persevere.

Perhaps you've heard the sarcastic saying, "No good deed goes unpunished." Have you ever done the right thing, only to be punished for it rather than rewarded? Has anyone ever lied about you or spread false rumors about you? Have you ever chosen to obey God's Word, but the results made it look as though His promises were not true? That's the Prison Test. That's what happened to Joseph. Joseph went through a long and very painful period when it looked as though there were no rewards for serving God. In that time, he learned to persevere.

Remember, God had a big destiny in mind for Joseph, and big destinies must be supported by big character. In order to walk in his destiny, Joseph was going to need the character trait of perseverance. And it was during the Prison Test that God gave Joseph the grace to persevere.

Jesus told us, "In the world you *will* have tribulation" (John 16:33, emphasis added). Jesus didn't say that you just *might* have tribulation. Jesus didn't say that some would have tribulation and others would not. No, Jesus said that as long as you are in this world, you *will* have tribulation. So you might as well get used to it.

You are probably familiar with Jesus' parable of the two houses in Matthew 7. Little children used to sing a song about it in Sunday School: "The wise man built his house upon the rock! The foolish man built his house upon the sand" (see Matt 7:24-27).

Well, there is something many people overlook about that parable: The storm came to both houses! Both the foolish man (the one who did not hear and obey the words of Jesus) and the wise man (the one who listened to and acted upon Jesus' words) experienced the same storm. The underlying truth here is this: Life is stormy because we live in a fallen world.

Whether you are saved or lost, righteous or wicked, saintly or sinful, the storms of life are going to come. Tribulation and trials will batter the house of your life from time to time. The question is, Will you allow them to do the work that God intends for them to accomplish in your life?

Joseph was in the midst of some serious tribulation. He had run away from sin, only to end up in a dungeon. That prison was probably a horrible place! But the penalty for attempted rape in Egypt at that time was death, so it was actually by the grace of God that Joseph ended up in that prison rather than in an early grave. I personally believe that Potiphar suspected his wife was lying. He was probably well aware of her true character, and he also knew the character of Joseph. So he spared Joseph's life. But he had to do something to save face, so he had Joseph thrown in prison.

The prison was under Potiphar's authority, since he was the captain of the guard. I like to believe that Potiphar put in a good word for Joseph, telling the keeper of the prison what a good servant Joseph was. But more than anything else, the choices that Joseph made in the prison caused him to be promoted there.

Although Joseph was suffering unjustly, he continued to do the right thing. Joseph didn't deserve to be in that dungeon, but he didn't let that stop him from doing his work "heartily, as to the Lord" (Col. 3:23). We know that is true, because the Bible tells us that Joseph was such a good steward that he ended up being promoted; soon he was in charge of the whole prison (see Gen. 39:22). And the Lord was with Joseph in the prison, making everything he did there prosper (see Gen. 39:23).

Here is the wonderful thing about Joseph. He didn't allow the injustice of his situation to stop the work of God in his life. No matter how difficult or unfair his circumstances seemed to be, Joseph allowed God to continue to use him. And it is absolutely essential that we learn to do that also. I have observed that some people are waiting for God to deliver them out of their unjust circumstances before they will do anything for Him. But if we are waiting for God to deliver us before we will serve Him, we will never do anything for God! Just like Joseph, we must allow God to use us *now*, whatever our circumstances might be—and trust in Him for the final outcome.

None of us likes the idea of experiencing tribulation. But if we look at the fifth chapter of Romans, we will see that God has some interesting things to say about tribulation.

> And not only that, but we also *glory in tribulations,* knowing that tribulation produces perseverance; and perseverance, character; and character, hope. Now hope does not disappoint, because the love of God has been poured out in our hearts by the Holy Spirit who was given to us (Rom. 5:3-5, emphasis added).

In verse 3, Paul says we "*glory* in tribulations." What does he mean by that word, "glory"? The Greek word for "glory" in this verse can be translated as "rejoice."[1] So this Scripture passage is saying that we *rejoice* in tribulation. That's right. We *rejoice* in it. (When I preached about this in a church service, I heard someone remark, "Yeah, right!" Of course, that kind of disbelief is a pretty natural response.)

But if we go deeper in the Greek, we can find out even more of what God has to say about tribulation. The root of the Greek word translated as "glory" is a word that basically means "to wish" or desire.[2] So this verse is not only telling us that we are to *rejoice* in tribulation, but it is also saying that we are to actually *desire* it!

How could we ever reach a point where we would actually *wish* for tribulation—and then rejoice in it when it comes? I believe the answer can be found in understanding what God has said about the way tribulation works in our lives. According to the Word of God, tribulation produces some good things in us. So we can rejoice in tribulation—even wish for it—because we know what tribulation will produce.

So, let's take a look.

Tribulation Produces Perseverance

I've searched high and low in the Bible to find out all the ways that we can obtain perseverance. But in all my searching, I have discovered only one. That one thing is tribulation.

Romans 5:3 tells us that "tribulation produces perseverance." And according to the Bible, there is no other way to get it. So why not allow that tribulation to produce perseverance, as God says it will? Why not allow that tribulation to do a valuable work of God in our lives?

In John 15, Jesus talks about two vines. One vine produces fruit, and the other vine does not. The vine that doesn't produce fruit gets cut off; and the vine that produces fruit gets pruned, or "cut on." There doesn't seem to be a whole lot of difference, does there? Both vines end up getting cut (see John 15:1-2).

Of course, if I have to choose, I would much rather be cut on than cut off. The point is that in either case, you can expect to be cut. If you do badly, you'll be cut off, or disciplined. If you do well, you'll be cut on, or pruned back, so you can bear more fruit. So whether we do the right thing or the wrong thing, we are going to experience some "cutting" times.

That is what happened to Joseph. He did the right thing, and he ended up being cut on. He made the right decision, so he ended up being "pruned." But God had a plan for that pruning. God's plan was that Joseph would one day bear more fruit.

This is why James said: "My brethren, count it all joy when you fall into various trials, knowing that the testing of your faith produces patience" (Jas. 1:2-3).

If there is one thing that we all understand about patience it is this: We all want patience. And we all want it *now!* But patience doesn't come that way. The only way we're going to get patience is through "the testing of our faith." And that is why we can "count it all joy" when we are going through a trial. That is why we can actually rejoice when we are being cut on. We can say, "Thank You, Lord, for this time of pruning, and this time of testing. You have said that this is going to produce something good in me. You have said that this will produce patience. So when I come out of this trial, I am going to have more of the fruit of the Spirit, and I am going to look more like Jesus."

This is how we glory in tribulation.

Patience can be described as waiting with contentment. And that is different from simply waiting. All of us will have to wait sometimes. But we all know that it is possible to wait and not be patient. It is possible to wait and not be content.

I can think of a good example from my own life to illustrate what I am talking about. When I go to the drive-through window at the bank, it seems that I have a special knack for getting in line behind the slowest person ever to make a financial transaction. First they take an eternity to put their items in the tube. And then, when the tube comes back, they seem to play with it for a while—before filling it with yet more items and sending it on for what seems like another endless journey to the teller and back! I'm not sure why, but this little ritual has a unique way of exasperating me to no end. Now God is still working in my life, but at this point, I am still working on "waiting with contentment"! I am still developing the fruit of the Spirit, which is patience, because when patience has had its perfect work in me, I will not only wait in that line, but I will also wait in that line "with contentment."

Patience is waiting with contentment. And the Bible says the testing of our faith is what works patience in us (see Jas. 1:2-3).

Perseverance demands that you fight the good fight of faith while you wait.

Yet there is a difference between patience and perseverance. Perseverance is similar to patience, in that perseverance also involves waiting. But perseverance involves more than just waiting with contentment. Perseverance involves *fighting the battle* while you're waiting with contentment. Perseverance demands that you fight the good fight of faith while you wait.

Perseverance takes longer than patience. You are not going to get perseverance in a week. The only way you get perseverance is by going through a long, difficult trial. You can have patience for 30 minutes in line at the bank. You can have patience for a week or for a month. But if a trial goes on for a long time, it takes more than patience to endure. It takes perseverance.

When the trial you are going through seems to go on forever, when months turn into years and still you must stand in faith—that is the test of perseverance. When the enemy attacks you with thoughts of doubt and hopelessness, that is the test of perseverance. And you must fight the good fight of faith during this test.

Joseph's first trial lasted 13 long years. For 13 years it looked as though God had forgotten him. For 13 years he had to battle his negative thoughts and keep his focus on God. For 13 years he had to keep on believing that what God had said was true. He had to have patience while the trial went on year after year. But he had to do more than just wait with contentment. He had to wait with an earnest faith in God. That is perseverance.

Joseph was not the only Bible character who had to persevere. David was anointed king of Israel, but it was 13 years before he assumed the throne as king. Paul was anointed as an apostle, but it was 13 years before his first missionary journey. (Once, when I had just preached on this subject, a woman came up to me after the service to tell me she, too, had waited 13 years—to have a child. She said, "I couldn't believe my ears when you said, '13 years'!")

If 13 years sounds like a long time, remember that Abraham had to wait 25 years for the son God had promised. And Moses had to wait 40 years in the wilderness before he stepped into his destiny.

Joseph could have become bitter toward his brothers; he could have become bitter toward the Egyptians; and he could have become bitter toward God. But instead Joseph kept his heart right, he kept his focus on God, and he persevered. And that perseverance resulted in character.

Perseverance Produces Character

You see, while tribulation produces perseverance, perseverance produces character. And character can only be developed through perseverance.

Just as I could find nothing in the Bible other than tribulation that produces perseverance, I could find nothing other than perseverance that produces character.

Now I would love to get perseverance, and get it right now. And it is much the same way with character. It would be great if I could simply go to someone who has character, have him or her lay hands on me and then instantly receive character. But it doesn't work that way. You can't get character by having someone pray for you or lay hands on you. Character must be *developed* on the inside of you. Character is only developed through perseverance. And perseverance only comes by endur-ing tribulation.

Isn't this an encouraging message? Perhaps not to our flesh.

But it is an important message, because character is absolutely essential in supporting the destiny God has in mind for you. And in order to develop that character, you're going to have to go through difficulties.

God will not allow you to step into your destiny until you have char-acter—a certain level of character. Because when you do step into your destiny, the warfare against you is going to increase. You will need strong character to endure that warfare, to persevere and to walk that destiny out to the end. Without character, you will never succeed in the destiny God has planned for you.

We all like the idea of instant rewards. But one of the worst things someone else could do for us would be to promote us before we have the character that is needed to handle that responsibility, or to deliver us out of a trial before God has achieved His goals in our character through it. Of course, none of us likes to go through a trial. But if we want to step into our destiny, we will have to go through that trial and allow God to develop His character in us.

Sometimes when we see someone going through a hard time, we want to rush right in and deliver him or her out of it. This is especially true of well-meaning Christians. Don't get me wrong—quite often we are simply responding in the love and compassion of God. But there are times when God is trying to use a situation to teach His children some-thing important, something they need to know for their destiny. It could have to do with managing their finances, or possibly even their relation-ships. And if a good, well-meaning Christian comes along and delivers them out of that difficulty, they will never learn the lesson God wants them to learn. Then they eventually end up right back in that same cri-sis situation again. And they have to keep retaking that test until they pass it!

Even Jesus had to learn by going through trials. Hebrews 5:8 says this about Jesus: "Though He was a Son, yet he learned obedience by the things which He suffered."

People often wonder about the meaning of that Scripture passage. After all, we know Jesus is the Son of God. And since Jesus is God, He is omniscient. That means He knows everything. But this verse says that Jesus, the Son of God, "learned obedience" (Heb. 5:8). How could Jesus, who knows everything, *learn* anything? And how could Jesus, who never sinned, learn *obedience?*

We must remember that although Jesus is the Son of God, He came to earth as a man. As a man He suffered, just like we do. As a man, He was tempted in every way that we are. And as a man, He learned obedience through the things He suffered.

The Bible tells us, "He Himself has suffered, being tempted" (Heb. 2:18). It also says He "was in all points tempted as we are, yet without sin" (Heb. 4:15).

You see, as the Son of God in heaven, Jesus didn't have to learn obedience. He was the Son of God, and He was perfect. There was no fleshly body to tempt Him to sin. But as a man, He had to go through trials. As a man, He was tempted to sin, and He had to overcome those temptations.

The deeper we go into the destiny God has planned for us, the deeper the character that will be required.

I'm not saying that Jesus wasn't perfect when He was on this earth. He was. He was fully God while He walked this earth. But it is important to remember that He was also fully man. As a man, He had to suffer. And *as He suffered, He learned obedience.*

Obedience is a character issue, and character can only be learned. It cannot be imparted. We are not born with character. Character is learned and developed as we are subjected to adversity. And this verse shows us that even Jesus Christ Himself developed character as a man and learned through the things He suffered.

The deeper we go into the destiny God has planned for us, the deeper the character that will be required. And the only way that deep character is produced is through deep trials. A person who has shallow character has only been through shallow trials. A person who has deep character has been through deep trials.

Now, please don't become fearful and start wondering what awful trial God has up His sleeve. God is not going to send you a trial—it's just going to happen! Remember, Jesus said, "In the world you *will* have tribulation" (John 16:33, emphasis added). So as long as you are on Earth, trouble will happen. That's just a part of life on this planet. So make the most of your tribulation: Allow whatever trial you are going through right now to produce godly character in you.

One way that deep trials work in our lives is by causing deep character flaws to emerge. We can see that happening in Joseph's situation. Why do you suppose Joseph had to go through such a long and difficult trial? I believe God wanted to work in a deep part of Joseph's character.

Joseph was not only a man with God's blessing and favor upon his life, He also had tremendous God-given leadership ability. If you look at Joseph's life, you can see that he rose to a position of authority in every situation, whether as a slave, as a prisoner or as the ruler of all Egypt. Obviously Joseph had a special ability to make whatever he was involved with a success. While it was the favor of God that made Joseph the ruler of Egypt, it was the natural ability God had given him that equipped him to handle that job! God had given Joseph a special gift. And when you have a special gift, it is easy to lean on that gift rather than on God.

While Joseph was in the prison, he used God's gift to interpret the dreams for the butler and the baker. Then he asked the butler to remember him when he returned to Pharaoh's court (see Gen. 40:8-15). But the butler forgot Joseph, and it took two more years before Joseph was delivered out of that prison (see Gen. 40:23; 41:1).

Why did it take two more years? Let's read the story.

And Joseph said to [the butler], "This is the interpretation of it: The three branches are three days. Now within three days Pharaoh will lift up your head and restore you to your place, and you will put Pharaoh's cup in his hand according to the former manner, when you were his butler. But remember me when it is well with you, and please show kindness to me; make mention of me to Pharaoh, and get me out of this house. For indeed I was stolen away from the land of the Hebrews; and also I have done nothing here that they should put me into the dungeon" (Gen. 40:12-15).

Do you know why the butler forgot Joseph? I believe God made the butler forget—because Joseph was trying to manipulate his circumstances. God moved through Joseph, giving him the interpretation of the dreams for the butler and the baker. But then Joseph jumped in with his own concerns and added, "Hey, put in a good word for me when you get out of here." I believe that when Joseph did that, God said, "Oops! Two more years! Because if I reward you now, you'll think the way to get ahead is to drop hints. If I deliver you now, you'll think that man promoted you and got you out of prison. So I'll let you wait two more years. Then you'll know I am the One who promoted you and delivered you."

It was "at the end of two full years" that Pharaoh had a dream (Gen. 41:1). And it was through interpreting Pharaoh's dreams that Joseph was finally delivered from the prison to the palace. Now, we know God gave Pharaoh those dreams to show him what was about to happen. So why didn't God give Pharaoh the dreams two years earlier? Why would God allow Joseph to endure two more years in that dungeon?

I believe there was a deep character flaw in Joseph, and God wanted that character flaw to emerge. That character flaw in Joseph was a tendency to trust in his own abilities. God had planned for Joseph to become the ruler of all Egypt and the instrument of God's provision during the famine. But in order for Joseph to rule as God's chosen vessel, he had to learn to lean totally on God—not on his own wisdom or ability.

Self-confidence, self-reliance and self-sufficiency all had to be dealt with before Joseph could step into his destiny. In the midst of that deep trial, Joseph learned that his own abilities would not be enough to get the job done.

That is the same lesson that we often have to learn. And it is only in the midst of deep trials that we start to see things from God's perspective. We come to a deeper understanding of who we really are and of who God is. We learn to respond correctly when troubles come. That is the way perseverance produces character in our lives.

Have you ever done the right thing, but suffered the wrong consequences? Have you ever been accused of something you didn't do? Have you ever been lied about or had rumors spread about you? I didn't really need to ask those questions, because I'm sure everyone could answer, "Yes!"

Everyone experiences hardship and injustice. But the hard times and the unjust situations we experience are not the deciding factors in our lives. The most important issue in our lives is *the way we respond* to those trials when they come. When we respond to those trials in the right way, character is being developed in our lives. *And character is simply doing the right thing in the wrong situation.*

And as character is developed, something wonderful happens. We begin to have hope.

Character Produces Hope

When you respond the right way to a wrong situation, something happens to your perspective. You start to see the bigger picture—and you start to see what God has in mind for your life. Suddenly, God looks much bigger than that trial or that problem. And this is how character works to produce hope. Hope sees things from God's perspective, no matter how the circumstances might look.

More than once Joseph did the right thing and suffered the wrong results. Thanks to Satan, Joseph often ended up on the receiving end of some injustice. But do you notice that Satan never had any new tricks? He used the same tactics on Joseph more than once.

First he used Joseph's coat to fabricate evidence that Joseph had been killed by wild animals (see Gen. 37:31-32). Later he used Joseph's coat to fabricate evidence that Joseph had attempted to rape Potiphar's wife (see Gen. 39:12-15).

As a young man, Joseph was just trying to do a good job for his father, Jacob, and he ended up being thrown into a pit (see Gen. 37:13-14,23-24). Later, he was just trying to be a faithful steward for Potiphar, and he was thrown in prison (see Gen. 39:20).

Joseph interpreted his dream for his brothers, and they sold him into slavery and forgot about him (see Gen. 37:6-10,24-30). Years later he interpreted a dream for the butler. But the butler went back to the palace and forgot about him (see Gen. 40:23).

He continued wearing coats (I think!). He continued doing a good job. And he continued interpreting dreams, which opened the door for him to step into his destiny!

Joseph could have become bitter many times. But instead he kept his heart right and responded in the right way to those wrong situations. He kept his focus on God through it all, and he persevered. That perseverance developed character in Joseph, which helped him to see things from God's perspective. And seeing things from God's perspective produced hope in Joseph's heart.

And here is the great thing about Joseph: *He didn't allow his hope to turn to disappointment.* Joseph's trial lasted for 13 long years. After the first 11 years had gone by, he interpreted the butler's dream—and when the dream came true, Joseph probably thought his deliverance had finally come. I'm sure he was looking forward to being released from that prison any day. But then days turned into weeks, and weeks turned into months—and months finally turned into two more years! Joseph had a perfect opportunity to become disappointed, but he kept his hope in God.

Of course, we know what the Word says about hope: "Hope deferred makes the heart sick, but when the desire comes, it is a tree of life" (Prov. 13:12).

Deferred hope is hope that has turned into disappointment. When you are going through a long and difficult trial, you must not allow that to happen. You must keep trusting God and hoping in Him. You must persevere and allow Him to show you His perspective—because if you allow your hope to turn to disappointment, your hope will be deferred. And God says that if you allow your hope to be deferred, you will end up with a sick heart.

Joseph's hope was deferred for 13 long years. If he had allowed those disappointments to rob him of his hope, he would have had a sick heart. Such a malady could have caused him to die before reaching his destiny. But Joseph did not allow his heart to become sick; rather, he kept his hope and trust in God alive.

Hope is for now. Hope is not just for the future. Hope is for the present! No matter what trial you might be in right now, even if you are in a dungeon, hope says God is right there with you. God is with you *now*.

I have observed that there is a tendency in some churches to continually preach about a move of God that is still to come. This bothers me, because they are not really preaching hope. They seem to have overlooked the reality that we are living in a move of God right now.

People must know that we don't have to wait for a move of God in the future. We are in a move of God right now! We have been in a move of God since Jesus Christ came to the earth. *Right now* you can have deliverance! *Right now* you can have healing! *Right now* you can have the gifts of the Holy Spirit! You don't have to wait for some move of God in the future. God is moving in the earth right now!

I know there are times of special outpourings of the Holy Spirit. But we need to thank God for what His Spirit is pouring out in our lives *right now*. If we continually look to the future, our hope will be deferred. And God says that deferred hope will make our hearts grow sick (see Prov. 13:12).

Hope is right now!

Hope is believing that God is working everything for our good *right now*.

Hope is believing that God loves us and that He is going to take care of us *right now*.

Hope is believing we're in the center of God's will—so we can have peace and joy *right now*.

Hope is believing God is with us *right now*, no matter what trial we might be going through.

That is biblical hope. That is not deferred hope. And character produces that kind of hope.

And guess what hope produces?

Hope Produces Appointments

Romans 5:5 tells us what hope does *not* do: *"Hope does not disappoint"* (emphasis added).

Let's look at that word "disappoint." To "dis" means "to undo" something. To "disappoint" means the opposite of "to appoint." So the word "disappointment" means that an appointment has been missed. If you say, "I was disappointed," it means that you missed an appointment. And if you missed an appointment, that could explain why you are disappointed!

If "hope does not disappoint" (Rom. 5:5), then what does hope do? That's easy—hope appoints! Hope produces appointments for you. And the appointments hope produces are *divine appointments*. They are appointments for you to minister to others and see their lives change, as well as your own. But without hope, you could become caught up in the trial you are going through and miss those divine appointments.

Joseph had a divine appointment in his future. But he could have missed that appointment if he had allowed his hope to turn to disappointment.

Joseph could have been having a pity party for himself every day. After all, he was in a very unjust situation, and it didn't look as though there was any way out. But instead of feeling sorry for himself, he kept his heart right. He kept looking for opportunities to minister. He didn't let that hopeless situation prevent him from reaching out and ministering to the needs of others. Joseph looked for divine appointments every day, right there in the prison. "And Joseph came in to them in the morning and looked at them, and saw that they were sad. So he asked Pharaoh's officers who were with him in the custody of his lord's house, saying, 'Why do you look so sad today?'" (Gen. 40:6-7).

Joseph was able to notice that the butcher and the baker were sad, because he had not allowed his own problems to consume him. In spite of his troubles, Joseph had persevered and allowed character to produce hope in his heart. And because he had hope in his heart, Joseph wasn't focusing on himself. He was looking to see how he could minister to someone else. Ironically, it was his ministry to one of his fellow prisoners that would eventually be the key to Joseph's deliverance!

Like Joseph, you must keep your hope in God, no matter what you are going through. You must remember that He has divine appointments for you every day. There are people all around you who need God, and God wants you to minister to those people. But if you focus only on your own problems and your own trials, you will walk right past opportunities to minister to the needs of others. You will miss appointments that are important to God. And if you miss an appointment that is important to God, you miss an appointment that is important to your destiny.

Here is my point: Joseph's brothers tried to thwart his destiny. Potiphar's wife tried to thwart his destiny. Then the butler messed it up. All those people did things which seemed certain to thwart God's plan for Joseph and to prevent him from entering into his destiny. But in spite of all those people, Joseph kept doing the right thing. And because he kept doing the right thing, Joseph didn't miss his divine appointment.

You must understand this truth. There is only one person who can thwart your destiny. There is only one person who can hinder you from reaching your destiny. There is only one person who can delay your destiny. Anyone want to take a guess? You. You're the only one.

I have accepted the fact that no one except me can mess up the destiny that is on my life. Just like you, I have others do things to me and say things about me that are wrong. I realize that if I don't respond in the right way to those injustices, I can mess up God's plan for my life. But I also know that if I choose to do what is right, there is nothing anyone else can say or do that will interfere with the plans God has for me! And if you choose to do what is right, no one else can stop the destiny that God has for you.

In the same way, no one else could interfere with Joseph's God-given destiny. Without a doubt, Joseph is a wonderful example for us of how we can persevere and come through tribulation with character and hope.

And Joseph is also a type of Christ.

Joseph went to prison for something he didn't do. Christ suffered for something he didn't do.

Joseph was numbered with the criminals in the prison. The Bible says Jesus "was numbered with the transgressors" (Isa. 53:12).

Joseph was jailed with two prisoners. One was set free, and one was condemned (see Gen. 40:21-22). Jesus was crucified between two thieves. One received forgiveness, and one did not (see Luke 23:33,39-43).

Joseph said to the butler, "Remember me when it is well with you, and please show kindness to me; make mention of me to Pharoah and get me out of this house" (Gen. 40:14), but the butler forgot about him. The thief said to Jesus, "Remember me when You come into Your kingdom" (Luke 23:42), but Jesus did not forget about him. Jesus remembered him that very day, as he was with Jesus in heaven (see Luke 23:43).

Here is my word for you: Even if other people don't keep their word, even if other people forget you, God never will. God will always keep His Word, and He will always remember you.

So when you are going through a long and difficult trial, allow that trial to produce perseverance in you. Keep fighting the good fight of faith as you wait with contentment for God's deliverance.

And as you allow God to develop His character in your life, you will start to do the right thing, no matter how wrong your situation is. You will start to see things from God's perspective. From His perspective, that trial is just a "light affliction, which is but for a moment"; from His perspective, that trial is working in you to produce "a far more exceeding and eternal weight of glory" (2 Cor. 4:17).

His perspective will cause you to always have hope.

And His hope will not disappoint you. It will carry you to a divine appointment with your destiny.

CHAPTER SIX

THE PROPHETIC TEST

Have you ever thought about how it is that God goes about creating something? Does He just wave His mighty hand? Or does He dream about something and then it automatically comes into being? We know that God is the Creator of all things. He has created each one of us, and that means that He is the Creator of our destinies as well. And the Bible tells us very plainly how it is that God creates. When God wants to create something, He *speaks*.

In the very first chapter of Genesis we read that when God wanted to create the heavens and the earth, He *spoke* and said, "Let there be light" (Gen. 1:3). When God wanted to create the animals, He *spoke* and said, "Let the earth bring forth the living creature according to its kind" (Gen. 1:24). And when He wanted to create man, God *spoke* and said, "Let Us make man in Our image" (Gen. 1:26).

Hebrews 11:3 tells us, "The worlds were framed by the word of God, so that the things which are seen were not made of things which are visible."

So everything that God has created, He has created by the words of His mouth. God brings things to pass by *speaking*.

In John 1, God says: "In the beginning was the Word, and the Word was with God, and the Word was God. All things were made through Him [the Word], and without Him [the Word] nothing was made that was made" (John 1:1,3). In this verse, God tells us that He and His Word are one. And the next thing He tells us is that "all things" were made through His Word (v. 3). (Obviously, "the Word" refers to His Son, Jesus. But notice, He calls His own Son "the Word.") Then, just in case that wasn't clear enough, God also lets us know that without His Word, "nothing was made that was made" (v. 3). In other words, everything that is made is made by God's words—and if it isn't made of God's words, it simply doesn't exist!

So when God wants to make something, He *says* it. When God has a plan for something, He speaks it forth. And when He speaks it forth, power is released for that thing to be created.

God had a plan for Joseph's life—so surely God had already spoken over Joseph's life before Joseph had the dreams. Before Joseph ever endured a test, God had already spoken regarding the final outcome He had planned. And long before Joseph stepped into his destiny, the power of God's words had already been released to carry him toward that destiny.

God has a plan for every one of us, just as He did for Joseph. And as we have just seen, when God has a plan for something, He *speaks*. That means that God has *already spoken* His plan over every one of us. He has *already spoken* a specific word over your life, and He has *already spoken* a specific word over mine. And when He spoke, the power was released to carry each one of us toward the destiny He has planned.

The Prophetic Test: Finding God's Word for Our Lives

God has called each of us for a specific purpose. There is no one else who can do what God has called you to do; there is no one else who can do what God has called me to do. But it is up to us to find out the specific words God has spoken over our lives. And it is up to us to believe the prophetic words that God has spoken, and then obey Him.

Will we believe God's words and stand on them, come what may? This is the Prophetic Test—the test of God's word.

God had spoken a word over Joseph's life. But Joseph went through some tough times when it seemed as though God's words and God's plans would never come to pass. In those times, Joseph was tested *by the words God had spoken over him*. Would he believe God's words—or the words of despair and hopelessness that his circumstances seemed to confirm?

The Bible describes how Joseph experienced this test: "He sent a man before them—Joseph—who was sold as a slave. They hurt his feet with fetters, he was laid in irons. Until the time that his word came to pass, the word of the LORD tested him" (Ps. 105:17-19).

It says here that they hurt Joseph's feet with fetters and that he was laid in irons (see Ps. 105:18). So we know that Joseph experienced some real physical suffering during this trial. But it also talks about something else that tested Joseph's character. It says that "the word of the LORD" (Ps. 105:19) actually tested Joseph as well.

I want you to notice that in the English translation of this verse, the word "word" occurs twice. But in the original Hebrew, there are actually two completely different Hebrew words translated as "word." They carry two very different meanings. They are the Hebrew words *dabar* and *imrah*. This verse actually says, "Until the time that his [dabar] came to pass, the [imrah] of the LORD tested him" (Ps. 105:19).

Now let me explain something to you about these Hebrew words. The first word, "dabar," is used 1,441 times in the Old Testament and is the Hebrew term most frequently translated as "word." The word "dabar" means "a matter" that is spoken of.[1]

With that in mind, we can see this verse is actually saying, "Until the time that [the *word that was spoken* over Joseph's life] came to pass, the word of the LORD tested him."

The second Hebrew word for "word" is "imrah." The word "imrah" appears only 37 times in the Old Testament. It means "commandment," "speech" or "word" and refers to the very Word of God—the literal Word of God.[2] This word is not used very often in the Bible. Let me give you a few passages in which the word "imrah" is used.

The words of the LORD are pure words, like silver tried in a fur-
nace of earth, purified seven times (Ps. 12:6).

As for God, His way is perfect; the word of the LORD is proven;
He is a shield to all who trust in Him (Ps. 18:30).

Your word I have hidden in my heart, that I might not sin
against You (Ps. 119:11).

In each of these verses the Hebrew word "imrah" is used, and it refers
to the literal Word of God.

So what Psalm 105:19 is actually saying about Joseph is this: Until
the time that Joseph's *prophetic* word (or *spoken* word) came to pass, the
literal Word of God tested him.

Here is an important insight.

The prophetic word tends to test our *faith*. But the literal Word of
God tests our *character*. And the literal Word of God is the Bible. The
Bible is our standard. The Bible is the Word by which all other words
from God must be measured. And because of that, it is absolutely essential that we know the Word (the Bible) of God.

Right now, you are being tested by the Word of God. God has
declared His Word to you in the Bible, and that Word is testing you.
Whether you reach your destiny or fail to reach your destiny will be
directly related to how well you know God's Word, as revealed in the
Bible. I can't emphasize this enough: *You need to know the Word of God!*

I see believers all the time who are trying hard to make progress, but
they are not fulfilling their destiny. And the reason they are not making
any progress is really quite simple: They are violating Scripture! The sad
part is that they don't even know that they are violating Scripture. If you
never read the Bible, how will you know what it says? And if you don't
know what it says, how will you know how to live?

The only way to know what the Bible says is to read the Bible. The
only way to know what God has said is to read His Book. So read the

Bible, meditate on it, memorize it, and get to know it. Because when you study the Bible, you are studying God's words. As a friend of mine, Pastor Bill Leckie, says, "If you are a Christian, you might as well face it: sooner or later, you're going to have to read the Bible!"

When I got saved, I wanted to know as much as possible about the Bible. And I still do! Something in me just craves what is in that Book! I don't read many other books. I wish that I did, because people ask me all the time whether I have read this or that book—and I have read some good books. But there is something about *God's Book* that I just can't get away from. I can't seem to get enough of His Book.

When I prepare a message, I never have a problem coming up with Scripture passages for my message. My problem is that I always have too many Bible verses, and I have to leave some of them out. I study and study, and sometimes I end up with hundreds of verses, too many to share in a single message. So I'm always saying to myself, *I guess I can take this Bible quote out—or maybe that one. I suppose I can make this point with just these 4 verses, instead of these 47!*

That may seem excessive to some, but not to me—I simply love God's Book! Ever since I met Jesus Christ and He changed my life, I have wanted to know Him as intimately as I can. And He has revealed Himself to us in the Bible. The Bible is the book of His words and the book of His life. So I want to know as much as I can about the Bible, not because I am a minister but because I'm a Christian—because I have met Jesus Christ, and I want to know more about Him.

When I first got saved, I spent hours and hours reading the Bible. I wanted to know how Mark related to Lamentations and how Hosea related to Acts. I wanted to put the whole thing together as one book. So I used to read 10 chapters a day. If you read 10 chapters a day, you can go through the whole Bible in 4 months. It is very simple. You can go through the whole Bible 3 times in single year by just reading 10 chapters a day.

For years, I read 10 chapters a day, which takes me about an hour. But there were times when I would read 50 chapters a day, and that would take about 5 hours. There were a few times that I was able to read 100 chapters a day. I realize that not every person would be able to do that—I'm in vocational ministry, so my job allows me to spend a great deal of time in the Word. But anyone—including you—could read through the whole Bible in single year by reading just 3 chapters a day. The important thing is to get started somewhere and to spend time every day in the Word of God.

The Bible is the greatest book there is. The words of the Bible are "life to those who find them and health to a [person's] whole body" (Prov. 4:22, NIV). The words in the Bible are "gold" (Prov. 25:11). And God Himself has said, "I am watching to see that my word is fulfilled" (Jer. 1:12, NIV). The Bible is the Word of God!

We should spend time in the Bible—and spending time in the Bible is fun! I used to get those Bible trivia books; and every time they came out with a new one, I would get it. I was in traveling ministry at that time, so when Debbie and I were on the road, I would have her quiz me. They had the beginner section, the amateur section and the expert section. We'd be driving down the road, and she would ask me questions such as, "Who were Huz and Buz?" Now you might think that it's not very important to know the answer to that question—but it was interesting to me, because I just wanted to know everything I possibly could.

Then I would say to Debbie, "Name a chapter in the Bible, any chapter." She would randomly pick a chapter and say something such as, "Ezekiel 45." Then I would try to tell her what that specific chapter talks about. I wanted to memorize as much as I could. So if she asked me about a chapter and I couldn't tell her what it talked about, I would have her read it to me, and then I would try to focus on it.

Then I would say to Debbie, "Name a Scripture. I'll see if I can tell you what that chapter says, what the context is and if I can tell you some other cross-references relating to it." Then if she said, "Mark, chapter 7," I would try to tell her what happened in that chapter. I would try to tell her where that same story is found in Matthew and Luke, and whether it is in all four of the Gospels or just in the Synoptic Gospels. That may sound a bit extreme to some, but my love for the Bible was coming straight out of the hunger in my heart—because I wanted to know the Word of God.

My hunger for God's Word didn't spring from the fact that I was a minister. It came from the fact that I was a believer. Jesus Christ changed my life—and He gave me His written Word so that I could know Him better.

So if you want to know Him, get to know the Word of God. It's that simple.

If you want to reach your destiny, you must come to the place where you know and love the Bible.

I personally believe that any person who reaches his or her destiny in God will also be a person who knows His Word. So if you want to reach your destiny, you must come to the place where you know and love the Bible.

The Bible is God's Book. And until the time that your dream comes to pass, God's Book is testing you. God's Book is testing your character. God's Book is testing your faith. God's Book is building your faith. And God's Book, the Bible, is the book that will bring you to your destiny.

God Still Speaks Today

We are very blessed to have the Bible. You know, Joseph didn't have the written Word of God as we have. All Joseph had at that time was the word that God had put in his heart—the prophetic word of God. And since that was all he had, I believe he held on to that, as the word that God had given him. But we are doubly blessed today. We are blessed to have God's written Word in the Bible—that is our standard, and we must hold on to that. And we also are blessed to have God's prophetic word; we must hold on to that as well.

Let me repeat that. God has given us His prophetic word today, and we are to hold on to it—because God still speaks today!

If you have been a part of a theological or doctrinal system that says God doesn't speak today, I want you to know something very important—that idea simply does not agree with the Scriptures! God did not lose His voice 2,000 years ago. Why in the world would you pray if you couldn't get an answer to your prayers? God does speak today. He never says anything contrary to what He has already said in the Bible, but He does speak. He hasn't lost His voice.

I'm sorry to say that many seminaries today are teaching that God stopped speaking 2,000 ago. Unfortunately, that is also what I was taught in Bible college. I was taught that God said everything He's ever going to say through the Bible, and that He doesn't speak anymore. But it's not true. He does speak! He still speaks—and one way that He speaks to us is by speaking to our hearts.

I used to be an associate pastor with Pastor Olen Griffing at Shady Grove Church (which used to be Shady Grove Baptist Church). When God began to move in that church, Pastor Griffing was called in front of a credentials committee to be questioned—because God was moving, you see, and this was a serious problem to be addressed!

For three hours Pastor Griffing was grilled by this committee about the nature of the Holy Spirit, the gifts of the Spirit and whether God moves today. At the end of three hours, the committee asked him, "Do you believe that when a tongue is interpreted, or when someone prophesies, that God could be speaking through that person?"

"Yes, I do," Pastor Griffing replied. "I don't believe that it is always God that is speaking when that happens. But, yes, I do believe that God sometimes speaks in that way today."

"That is where we've got you!" they said. "After three hours, that is where we've got you—because the Bible contains everything that God has said, and He does not speak to us anymore. If you say that God told you something, and you can't give us 'chapter and verse' in the Bible, then you are adding to the Bible—and you know what happens when you add to the Bible."

Brother Griffing replied, "You men have been questioning me for three hours now, and I've been answering your questions. Now may I ask each of you one question?" After the gentleman agreed, he said, "You're telling me that God doesn't speak today. So I have just one question for you. If God doesn't speak today, then who called you to preach?"

At that, all five committee members began looking at their shoes. They had nothing to say. So Pastor Griffing addressed the chairman of the committee. "Dr. So-and-So, I asked you a question. Who called you to preach?"

Dr. So-and-So cleared his throat—and then reluctantly answered, "God did."

"Good," said Brother Griffing. "Would you mind giving me 'chapter and verse' in the Bible for that?"

But Dr. So-and-So had no reply.

So Brother Griffing said, "It is obvious that God must speak today—because He spoke to you in your heart when He called you to preach. We know that God never says anything contrary to this Bible—but He does speak today."

That was a word of wisdom that the Holy Spirit gave to Pastor Griffing for that moment. But in spite of that word of wisdom, they still kicked him out! Pastor Griffing didn't mind, though. He understood the truth that God still speaks today—and that if God is speaking, we shouldn't let anyone or anything talk us out of it!

The apostle Paul must have encountered a problem similar to Pastor Griffing's, because he wrote to the church at Thessalonica: "Do not quench the Spirit. Do not despise prophecies. Test all things; hold fast what is good" (1 Thess. 5:19-21).

According to the Bible, God does have some things to say to us today through prophecies. And we are not to "despise" those prophecies. If we do, Paul says that we run the risk of "quenching" the Holy Spirit Himself.

Of course, God speaks to us in His written Word, and we must always hold on to what He has said in His written Word—the Bible is our standard. But according to this verse of Scripture, God also speaks to us through the prophetic word. And we are commanded to "hold fast" to those prophetic words.

If we are to hold on to the prophetic word of God, there are some important things about the prophetic that we must understand. One thing we must understand is that prophetic words are only a part of what God is saying.

Prophetic Words Are Only a Part of the Puzzle

There are many verses about prophecy in chapters 12 through 14 of 1 Corinthians. And 1 Corinthians 13:9 has this to say: "For we know in part and we prophesy in part." This verse says that, "we know in part"—which just means that we don't know everything. God knows everything, but we don't. We only know a part of everything. And since we don't know everything, our prophecy isn't everything. Our prophecy is just a part of everything. That is why "we prophesy in part" (13:9). Since what we know is just a part of the bigger picture, our prophecy can only be a part of that bigger picture.

The bigger picture is just like a puzzle. God knows the whole puzzle—He designed it! But we know only a part of the puzzle. And since we know only a part of the puzzle, our prophecy is only a part of the puzzle. It is not the whole picture—it is just a part.

If you were perfect, you could prophesy perfectly—but none of us is perfect. Only God is perfect. And there is always a human element to prophecy. The Bible tells us, "The spirits of the prophets are subject to the prophets" (1 Cor. 14:32). So we have to take the prophetic word and consider it in light of the bigger picture.

God has given us prophetic words to encourage us and to cause us to seek Him. But prophetic words are not the whole picture. That is why we must take the prophetic word God has spoken to us and submit it to the bigger Word God has spoken in His Book. His Book is the perfect Word of God. When we put the prophetic word God has spoken to us together with His perfect written Word, we will come up with a more complete picture of what God is saying.

I can think of a story that is a good illustration of how this works.

On the last day of December, it is not uncommon for me to have a prophetic dream regarding the coming year. This does not happen every year, but there are certain years when this has occurred. (I think it depends on what I eat that night—just kidding!)

Years ago I had just such a dream on New Year's Eve. In the dream, I was riding in a car with my friend Mark Jobe, who is an evangelist. A pastor friend of mine was in the driver's seat, I was in the middle, and Mark was sitting to my right, by the passenger door. All three of us were together in the front seat. (Is that in itself an indication that perhaps I had a little too much pizza?)

The three of us began to discuss what God was saying about the coming year. Mark had just preached a prophetic message that God had spoken to him. In Mark's message, God was saying that the coming year was going to be a year of darkness.

The pastor said, "You know, Mark, I don't want to argue with you at all. I'm really just trying to understand what God is saying. But I really believe God spoke to me also. And when God spoke to me, He said this was going to be a year of light."

Mark said quite pleasantly, "Well, I understand that, and I wouldn't want to disagree. But I really believe God spoke to me. And He said it is going to be a year of darkness."

"I certainly appreciate that," the pastor replied. "But I believe it is going to be a year of light."

Mark responded, "Well, I understand what you are trying to say, but . . ." And so the conversation went on and on. It wasn't an argument by any means; it was a discussion. But they kept going back and forth, and I was sitting in the middle watching them, as if I were watching a tennis match.

Then suddenly I broke in. "Guys, don't you understand? Don't you remember the story in the Bible about the ninth plague in Egypt? Darkness covered the whole land—but the children of Israel had light in their dwelling places. So both of you are right! God is saying that it is going to be a year of darkness for those who are not following Him; and a year of light for those who are following Him."

When I woke up from that dream, I knew the Lord had just spoken to me about the coming year. I even preached that prophetic word that very year!

Here is my point: In the dream, each man had a part of what God was saying. And it was only by putting the parts together that the full message of God could be understood.

It is important that we understand this, because all too often we choose the prophecies that we like, and we only listen to those. Or we choose the pastors or ministers we like, and we only listen to them. But all of the ministry gifts have a part in God's puzzle—and if we leave some out, we won't see the full picture.

When we're listening to different ministers of God, on the television for example, we shouldn't tune in to watch only those who strike the "right chord" for us at that moment. Instead, we ought to be asking, "God, what are You saying through that preacher? And what are You saying through this one? And what are You saying through that man?" We need to take heed of all of the ministry gifts, because they are all pieces of the puzzle.

Because God wants us to follow Him by faith, He often does not tell us everything or show us the whole picture.

If we had heard those two prophecies from my dream, we might be tempted to see which one suits our fancy. "Let's see, now. A year of darkness, and a year of light. Hmm. I think I like that one about a year of light. Yes, I think that one about a year of light is from the Lord! That is God's word for me!" If we do that, we are embracing one prophecy and ignoring the other. Yet God is speaking through both.

As humans, we know only "in part"; therefore, we prophesy only "in part" (1 Cor. 13:9). So if you have a prophetic word, you must understand that it is not everything. It is only a part. And because God wants us to follow Him by faith, He often does not tell us everything or show us the whole picture.

Prophetic Words Are to Be Judged

In the fourteenth chapter of 1 Corinthians, Paul is talking about prophecies, and he says, "Let two or three prophets speak, and let the others judge" (1 Cor. 14:29).

This verse makes it clear that we are to allow prophecies to be spoken. But it also says that when those prophecies have been spoken, we are to *judge* them, or test them. Why? Because when humans speak under the prophetic influence, there will always be a human element involved. And it is up to us to discern, or "judge," what is truly the word of the Lord—and what is human influence. That is why the Bible tells us to judge prophecy.

Prophecy can be compared to pure water from a hose that is being sprayed through a window screen. God's words are the pure water, and our human spirits are the window screens. This illustration was given to me by a pastor after I had ministered prophetically at his church. After the meeting was over, he said to me, "Thank you for coming to my church with a clean screen."

"A clean screen?" I said to him. "I've never heard that expression. What do you mean by a clean screen?"

So he explained exactly what he meant.

Prophecy is like water that is coming out of a pure-water hose. It comes from God, and it is pure when it comes from God. It is pure when it comes from the hose. But we are like the window screen, and the water goes through us. Sometimes our screens are dirty. So even though the water is clean when it comes out of the hose, if there is dirt in our screen, the water will have some dirt in it when it comes out on the other side.

There are prophets who have come and ministered at my church, and their screens were judgmental. It was like they were hearing from God, but everything they were saying was tinted with harshness or judgment.

So when that pastor had said, "Thank you for coming with a clean screen," he was just thanking me for allowing God's prophetic words to flow to his congregation without mixing in "dirt" from my own personality or my own issues.

That pastor had learned to do what the Bible says to do: to judge prophecies (see 1 Cor. 14:29). And that is what we must learn to do with prophecies. We must learn to discern what is dirt from the screen and what is the pure word that comes from God.

How We Judge Prophecy

We Judge Prophecy by the Word of God

We must judge prophecy and test it. And the first way we judge prophecy is by holding it up to the Word of God. The Word of God is always our standard. God never contradicts Himself, so a true prophecy will never contradict the Word of God.

God makes this very plain in Deuteronomy 13. He warns us that there will be prophecies which contradict His Word, and that these false prophecies will sometimes even be accompanied by signs and miracles.

> If there arises among you a prophet or a dreamer of dreams, and he gives you a sign or a wonder, and the sign or the wonder comes to pass, of which he spoke to you, saying, "Let us go after other gods"—which you have not known—"and let us serve them," you shall not listen to the words of that prophet or that dreamer of dreams, for the LORD your God is testing you to know whether you love the LORD your God with all your heart and with all your soul (Deut. 13:1-3).

God is letting us know that we should never listen to a prophecy which contradicts His Word—even if that prophecy is accompanied by the prediction of a sign or miracle which comes to pass! If a prophecy contradicts God's Word, it is not a prophecy from God—because God never contradicts Himself! He never says one thing in His Word and something else through prophecy. That is why God's Word must always be our standard.

And God actually calls this a test (see Deut. 13:3). He says He is *testing* us in these situations. Will we love the Lord our God with all of our heart and with all of our soul? If we do, we will hold fast to His Word, no matter what. We will hold fast to His Word, and not to signs or miracles or false prophecies. We must judge every prophecy by the Word of God, allowing God's Word to be the final answer.

I never cease to be amazed at the fact that some people have actually told me, "God told me to do this" or "God told me to do that." And it is all too obvious that God never told them anything of the kind—because what they had been "told" to do was a clear violation of His Word! God is not going to contradict what He has said in the Bible.

We must go by the standard. And the standard is God's Word. The standard has nothing to do with whether someone gives you a prophetic word and you think that word is right. If that word doesn't line up with the Word of God, it is not right! Don't tell me God told you to do something which contradicts what the Bible says—He didn't. If it is contrary to the Scriptures, you have not heard the voice of God.

This is the prophetic test. Joseph had to take it and so do we: "Until the time that his word came to pass, the word of the LORD tested him" (Ps. 105:19).

No matter what you hear, no matter what you see, no matter what you experience, will you be faithful to the word that God has spoken? Will you hold fast to God's Word, no matter what trial you might be going through? Will you hold fast to God's Word, no matter what the circumstances might be saying?

We Judge Prophecy by the Inward Witness

Another way we judge prophecy is by the inward witness—by holding it up to what God is saying to us in our own hearts. After all, the Bible says, "The Spirit Himself bears witness with our spirit" (Rom. 8:16). That just means that our own human spirit can recognize the Spirit of God when He is talking. When our spirit recognizes the Holy Spirit, the Holy Spirit is bearing witness with our spirit. And the more we know God, the more readily we will recognize His voice.

There may be times when you receive a prophecy, but it just doesn't seem to agree with what God has been speaking to you personally. It doesn't contradict God's written Word, yet it just doesn't seem to line up with what the Holy Spirit has been speaking to you in your own spirit. If that should happen, don't be concerned about it. Just put that prophecy on the shelf. If that word is from God, He will eventually make that clear to you in your own spirit. And if it is not from God, it can just stay on that shelf!

Someone once asked me, "Aren't I supposed to be faithful to the prophecy?"

"No," I replied. "You're supposed to be faithful to God! Just stay faithful to Him. If you don't understand a prophecy, just tell God about it and give it to Him. Say, 'God I don't understand this right now. If this is Your word for me, I will embrace it. But for now, God, I choose to embrace *You*. I choose to trust in *You*. And I trust that every word that *You* have truly spoken will come to pass in my life.'"

Judge every prophecy by the Word of God and the faith of God.

In Jeremiah 35 there is a great example of a situation in which prophecy had to be judged by the inward witness. The Rechabites had received a word from their father, Jonadab, not to drink wine—and then they received another word that contradicted the first one (see Jer. 35:5-6). Were they to listen to the "prophet" Jeremiah? Or were they to hold fast to the word that their father had commanded them?

God had told Jeremiah to go set wine before the Rechabites and tell them to drink it (see Jer. 35:1-2). So Jeremiah obeyed God. He called the Rechabites, put wine in front of them and said, "Drink wine" (Jer. 35:5). What were the Rechabites to do? Their father had commanded them not to drink wine—but now, a true prophet of the Lord was commanding them to drink wine! Do you know what the Rechabites said to Jeremiah?

The Rechabites said, "You are telling us to drink wine, but that can't possibly be right. Because God already gave a word to our father, Jonadab, that we were not supposed to drink wine. God has already spoken to us about this" (see Jer. 35:6-8).

Jeremiah was a true prophet of the Lord, and he was obeying God by telling them to drink wine. But *this was a test*. And the word Jeremiah spoke to the Rechabites did not bear witness with them. It didn't contradict God's written Word. But it did contradict what God had *already told them to do* through their father Jonadab. And the prophetic word of their father Jonadab still witnessed with them as being the true word of God. So they judged the prophecy from Jeremiah, and they did not obey it. They obeyed the prophetic word that had first been given to them, and that word seemed right.

Then God said to Jeremiah, "Now you go and tell Israel about this. Tell them that the Rechabites are obeying the word that was given to them by their father—but you Israelites are not obeying the Words that I gave to your fathers" (see Jer. 35:12-14).

God told Jeremiah to do this in order to show us something. When God has spoken to us, we must hold fast to His Word and obey it. We must hold fast to His written Word, and we must also hold fast to his prophetic word. And we must judge every prophetic word by the Word of God and the witness of the spirit.

Every Word from God Is Submitted to the God of the Word

Remember, there is a human element to prophecy—because prophets are human beings speaking God's words to other human beings. And all words from God are submitted to the God of the Word. That means that every word of prophecy is submitted to God who has spoken it. Now can I blow your theology, just for a minute?

The Bible tells us of a true prophet who had a true word from God— *but that word did not come to pass!* That prophet was Jonah. I would say Jonah was definitely a true prophet, wouldn't you? After all, he did get his very own book of the Bible, and that's not bad! But Jonah spoke a true prophecy from God, and that prophecy did not come to pass. We tend to think that if someone is a true prophet, then all of his or her prophecies will come to pass. But that is not always the case, because *every word of God is submitted to the God of the Word.*

Jonah disobeyed God's command at first, but then later he obeyed. He went to Nineveh and said what God told him to say: "In forty days Nineveh will be destroyed" (see Jonah 3:4). Notice Jonah didn't say, "Repent, or you will be destroyed." No, he simply said, "Yet forty days, and Nineveh *shall* be overthrown!" (Jonah 3:4, emphasis added).

But 40 days went by, and guess what happened? Nineveh was not destroyed! Why? The word Jonah had spoken was a true word from God. But *all words from God are submitted to the God of the Word.* And when the people of Nineveh heard God's word, they decided they didn't want to be destroyed, and they repented. The Bible says that when they repented, "God relented from the disaster that He had said He would bring upon them, and He did not do it" (Jonah 3:10).

In other words, God changed His mind about what He had said He was going to do! When the people of Nineveh turned to God, God turned the prophecy.

You would expect that Jonah would have been glad to see that an entire city had been saved from destruction through his prophetic ministry. Jonah had obeyed God and spoken God's prophetic word to Nineveh; and as a result, the city had repented and was not destroyed. But Jonah was not happy about it. Instead, he was very angry—because now it looked as though he was a false prophet. Because of God's mercy on Nineveh, Jonah's prophecy had not come to pass!

Jonah even admitted to God that this was why he had refused to obey God in the first place and had fled to Tarshish.

> Therefore I fled previously to Tarshish; for I know that You are a gracious and merciful God, slow to anger and abundant in lovingkindness, One who relents from doing harm. Therefore now, O LORD, please take my life from me, for it is better for me to die than to live! (Jonah 4:2-3).

Because now it looked to the people of Nineveh as though Jonah was a false prophet, he had decided it would be better to die, rather than face the fact that the prophecy he had spoken did not come to pass. He was more concerned with the word God had spoken through him than with pleasing the God who had spoken it. I am sorry to say that I have been amazed to see this occur sometimes in those who move in the prophetic—they would rather be right about their prophecies than have a whole nation turn to God! (That was a pretty strong statement—wasn't it?)

Jonah's situation was not unusual. Isaiah was a true prophet of God—and yet Isaiah also spoke a word from God that did not come to pass. God sent Isaiah to King Hezekiah and told him to say, "Thus says the LORD: Set your house in order, for you shall die and not live" (Isa. 38:1).

That was a true word of prophecy from the Lord. But when Hezekiah heard that prophecy, he prayed and asked God to change His mind. Then the word of the Lord came a second time to Isaiah and said, "Go and tell Hezekiah, 'Thus says the LORD, the God of David your father: "I have heard your prayer, I have seen your tears; surely I will add to your days fifteen years"'" (Isa. 38:5).

The God of the Word is Love. His heart will always be made manifest through the words He speaks.

Because Hezekiah humbled himself and prayed, God had mercy on Hezekiah. God changed His mind, and He then spoke another word about Hezekiah's future—a word that was radically different from the first word. So the first true word of the Lord that Isaiah had spoken did not come to pass.

You see, every word of God is submitted to the God of the Word. And the God of the Word is full of mercy. The God of the Word is Love. His heart will always be made manifest through the words He speaks, and it is important that we remember that. We have to hold on to prophetic words, but we also have to judge prophetic words and test prophetic words. We judge them by the Word of God and the inward witness. And we stay submitted to the God who has spoken those words—because every word God has spoken is submitted to the God of the Word.

Hold On to Prophetic Words

Throughout our lives, we are going to encounter circumstances which contradict the words God has spoken over us. One of the most important things we can do if we want to pass the Prophetic Test is simply to hold on—hold on to the words God has spoken to us! Because there will be many opportunities to let go of those words or to stop believing that what God said is going to come to pass.

As I've said, God tests our faith with the prophetic word, and He tests our character with the written Word. We absolutely must hold on to those things God has spoken over our lives. And the way we hold on is by faith.

If God has spoken something to you, hold on to it! If God has said that you are going to do a certain thing for Him, hold on to it! Don't let it go, whatever may happen, and don't give up believing in the words God has spoken! Joseph could have given up, and let go of the things God had spoken about his destiny. But if Joseph had let go of those dreams, he never would have made it to the destiny to which God had called him. All through Joseph's trial, he had to hold on to the word of God. He had to keep on believing that the things God had spoken over his life would be fulfilled.

The apostle Paul understood the importance of holding on to the prophetic word of God. Remember what he wrote to the church at Thessalonica: "Do not despise prophecies. Test all things; hold fast what is good" (1 Thess. 5:20-21). Paul is telling them to test all prophecies and to hold fast to those prophecies that are good. Good prophecies are those that are from God.

If we are going to hold on to those prophecies, it is going to require some effort on our part. Paul described that effort as "pressing on." In Philippians 3:12, Paul says, "Not that I have already attained, or am already perfected; but I press on, that I may lay hold of that for which Christ Jesus has also laid hold of me."

Paul is talking about his destiny. He is saying that Jesus Christ has laid hold of him, for a specific purpose—and Paul wants more than anything to lay hold of that purpose. He wants more than anything to hold on to the things Jesus Christ has called him to do. He wants to hold on to the words God has spoken about his destiny. But Paul says that in order to do that, he has to *"press on"* (Phil. 3:12, emphasis added). In other words, he has to push forward, he has to resist, and he has to exert some effort if he is going to hold on to the words God spoke over his life.

Timothy was Paul's son in the faith, and Paul wrote to let Timothy know about this test and struggle that all of us must go through.

This charge I commit to you, son Timothy, according to the prophecies previously made concerning you, that by them you may wage the good warfare, having faith and a good conscience, which some having rejected, concerning the faith have suffered shipwreck, of whom are Hymenaeus and Alexander, whom I delivered to Satan that they may learn not to blaspheme (1 Tim. 1:18-20).

Paul is reminding Timothy of the prophecies that had been spoken over his life, and he is exhorting Timothy to hold on to those prophecies. Paul says it is *by those prophecies* that Timothy will "wage the good warfare, having faith and a good conscience." This is pretty amazing. According to Paul, holding on to that prophetic word is absolutely critical to Timothy's fulfilling God's call on his life. It is by holding on to the prophetic words of God that Timothy will wage warfare on the devil, keep his conscience clear and fight the good fight of faith!

What is possibly even more amazing is what Paul has to say about two young men who did not hold on to the prophetic words of God—Hymenaeus and Alexander. Paul says that these young men rejected the prophecies made over their lives, and because of that they suffered shipwreck—meaning they didn't reach their destination (destiny) in God (see 1 Tim. 19-20). Then Paul says that because they rejected God's word for their lives, he had turned them over "to Satan that they may learn not to blaspheme" (v. 20). It sounds to me like Paul is saying that rejecting a true word from God is blasphemous. These are pretty strong consequences for rejecting the prophetic word of God—"delivered to Satan" and "suffered shipwreck" (v. 19-20)—but that is what the Bible says!

Hold on to the word of God. If God has given you a word about your life, hold on to it. I want to say this again—there is only one person who can prevent you from walking into your destiny, and that person is you. So don't block your destiny. Hold on to the things God has spoken over your life.

Twenty-something years ago, God spoke to me about leaving an employer. When I left, that employer said to me, "You will never amount to anything if you leave me." But even as a young man, that didn't affect me at all. Do you know why it didn't affect me? Because God had spoken to me! So I just held on to what God had said.

Recently I had a little surprise as I was looking through some of my computer files. I came upon a file I had never seen before—it was titled "Elaine's First Prophecy." Now Elaine is my 14-year-old daughter, and without my realizing it, she had typed this up and saved it on my computer. Elaine had received her first prophecy and wanted to be sure to save it—apparently she was planning on getting some more!

I was somewhat blown away by this, I have to admit, and a bit humbled as well. Because here was a 14-year-old girl, holding on to the prophetic word she had received—yet so many adults do not. So many adults have let go of the things God has spoken over their lives. They have forgotten what God has said about their destiny—or simply have stopped believing in it. They have allowed the circumstances of their lives to cloud their vision and to convince them that the things God has said they will do for Him are never going to happen.

Don't let that be you. Hold on to the words God has spoken over your life, and believe Him! That is what I must do. That is what Elaine will have to do. And that is what you must do also, if you want to pass the Prophetic Test.

Until the time that the prophetic word of God comes to pass in your life, the written Word of God is testing you. So get to know His Word. Study the Bible; meditate on it; memorize it. Remember that knowing what God has said in His written Word is the key to seeing His prophetic words fulfilled in your life.

As you wait for the fulfillment of your destiny, keep in mind that there is only one Person you need to please, and that is God! As long as you serve Him, no one else can stop what He has planned for you!

God has a destiny for your life. He has someone He wants you to touch. He has someone He wants you to reach. He has a ministry for you (though it may not be a vocational ministry). So hold on to that destiny.

And hold on to the prophetic word of God, no matter what happens. Press on, and lay hold of those things God has promised. When you do that, you will pass the Prophetic Test. And one day you will step into your destiny. One day you will see every word that God has spoken over your life come to pass.

CHAPTER SEVEN

THE POWER TEST

When our daughter Elaine was a little girl, it was not uncommon for me to walk into a room and find all of her dolls neatly lined up, with Elaine dictating orders to them. She would say, "Now you go over there, and you go here; you do this, and you do that." What struck me the most about that scene was the way that even a small child could express the inward desire to rule over the world around her—even if her authority extended only to her dolls!

Has it ever occurred to you that the desire for power is just built into human nature—that it is a part of who God made us to be? It seems to me that human beings are just hardwired to want to rule and have dominion over the world around them. If you don't believe me, just get your children a dog. Dogs can really take a licking in the pecking order of family life—but especially from the youngest member of the house- hold, who is usually in the position of being ruled over by everyone else. It is amazing how even the smallest child will jump at the chance to finally have something to rule over or dominate. No matter how young, they don't seem to need any lessons in how to boss the dog around!

If we watch children, we quickly see that every person arrives on this earth with a desire to rule. To put it another way, we all have a desire for power. But where do we get that desire for power? We get it from God!

All too often we think of the desire for power only in negative terms. Of course, there is a wrong desire for power, a desire that is rooted in selfishness—but there is also a right desire for power. There is a desire for power that God has put into each human being when he or she was created. God is all-powerful, and the Bible tells us that He created humankind in His own image. So when we were created, we were created in the image of an all-powerful Ruler.

Genesis 1:27-28 tells the story.

So God created [humankind] in His own image; in the image of God He created [humankind]; male and female He created them. Then God blessed them, and God said to them, "Be fruitful and multiply; fill the earth and subdue it; have dominion over the fish of the sea, over the birds of the air, and over every living thing that moves on the earth."

God created humankind "in His own image"—and the very first thing He told Adam and Eve to do was to "have dominion" over the earth and to "subdue" it. So from the very beginning, God not only created us to have power, but also commissioned us to use it. He planned for us to have power and to use it the way He does—to do good and to make life on Earth better. We are made in the image of an all-powerful God, who uses His power to bless people, minister to people and help people.

The Power Test: Learning to Steward Your God-Given Authority

I know you may have never heard this before, but I am telling you that you actually have a legitimate desire for power in you—and this desire comes from God!

God created us to have power and He wants to give His power to us—but He is looking for those who can be trusted with His power. What will we do with the power He gives us? Will we use it wisely, as His stewards on this earth?

This is the Power Test.

So far most of the tests we've studied have involved the way we respond when bad things happen in our lives. But the Power Test is different. This test has to do with how we respond when something *good* happens.

How do you respond to success? How do you respond to power? How do you respond to authority? How do you respond to influence? How do you respond to God's blessings? It is what you do with the power and the blessings of God that is the true test of your character.

This may come as a surprise to some, but God's blessings can be just as much a test as tribulations can—because blessings involve responsibility, and responsibility requires character. If God blesses believers, and they don't have the character necessary to handle that blessing, they will fall or misuse that blessing for selfish reasons. That is why God spent so many years building Joseph's character before giving him the responsibility to rule over Egypt.

Every person will go through the Power Test, because every person has some degree of authority and responsibility. You might not think you have much authority—but if you think carefully, you will realize there is something God has given you responsibility over. It might be something as small as a puppy or as seemingly insignificant as a room full of dolls—but you have dominion over *something* in your life! And in that area of authority, you are being tested.

Since I am a pastor, an example that easily comes to my mind is a man who starts out serving in the church parking lot. Every week he is faithful in that responsibility, just following orders and parking cars "for Jesus." After a while his faithfulness becomes apparent to everyone, and eventually he is made the "parking lot captain." So the next week he shows up with a uniform, a bullhorn and a huge flashlight that looks like a prop from a *Star Wars* movie. That parking lot is now his place of responsibility!

The point I am trying to make is this: We all have responsibility over something, and everyone will be tested by that responsibility. How do you respond when you're given responsibility or authority? How do you handle that dominion? This is the essence of the Power Test. When

Joseph stepped out of the dungeon, he stepped into a place of great power and great authority—and he also stepped into the Power Test. Joseph was only stepping into the first part of the first phase of his destiny at that time. If Joseph had handled that power in the wrong way, he never would have been able to fulfill his destiny in the way God had planned.

Genesis tells the story of how Joseph was called from the dungeon to interpret Pharaoh's dreams. At that time Joseph had been in prison for 12 years; and it had been 2 full years since he had interpreted the dreams for the butler and the baker. But things were about to change.

> Then it came to pass, at the end of two full years, that Pharaoh had a dream; and behold, he stood by the river. Now it came to pass in the morning that his spirit was troubled, and he sent and called for all the magicians of Egypt and all its wise men. And Pharaoh told them his dreams, but there was no one who could interpret them for Pharaoh. Then the chief butler spoke to Pharaoh, saying: "I remember my faults this day." Then Pharaoh sent and called Joseph, and they brought him quickly out of the dungeon; and he shaved, changed his clothing, and came to Pharaoh (Gen. 41:1,8-9,14).

Not only did Joseph give Pharaoh the interpretation of his dreams, he also gave Pharaoh some free advice about how to prepare for the coming years of famine (see Gen. 41:25-36). And Joseph's advice was so full of wisdom that it caused Pharaoh to conclude that Joseph must be filled with the Spirit of God (see Gen. 41:38). (I find it interesting that three men who were unbelievers—Potiphar, Pharaoh and the keeper of the prison—all recognized that the Spirit of God was with Joseph.)

> So the advice was good in the eyes of Pharaoh and in the eyes of all his servants. And Pharaoh said to his servants, "Can we find such a one as this, a man in whom is the Spirit of God?" Then Pharaoh said to Joseph, "Inasmuch as God has shown you all this, there is no one as discerning and wise as you. You shall be

over my house, and all my people shall be ruled according to your word; only in regard to the throne will I be greater than you." And Pharaoh said to Joseph, "See, I have set you over all the land of Egypt." Then Pharaoh took his signet ring off his hand and put it on Joseph's hand; and he clothed him in garments of fine linen and put a gold chain around his neck. And he had him ride in the second chariot which he had; and they cried out before him, "Bow the knee!" So he set him over all the land of Egypt. Pharaoh also said to Joseph, "I am Pharaoh, and without your consent no man may lift his hand or foot in all the land of Egypt" (Gen. 41:37-44).

In a single day, God can suddenly change everything about your circumstances! In one day God can bless you and put you into your destiny.

So the Pharaoh gave Joseph his signet ring, which represented his rights and authority as the ruler of Egypt. He clothed Joseph in fine linen and put a gold chain around his neck, representing the riches that Joseph would now enjoy. And he had Joseph ride in his chariot, with people crying out, "Bow the knee!" as he went by—which represented the royal position in which Joseph now stood. He had the three Rs—rights, riches and royalty. Now, that's *power!* In what must have seemed like the blink of an eye, Joseph found himself in the middle of the Power Test!

The Power Test Comes Suddenly

This is often the way it happens with the Power Test. It comes suddenly. Just like Joseph, you may work hard for 10, 15 or 20 years—and then, in a single day, God can suddenly change everything about your circumstances! In one day God can bless you and put you into your destiny.

That is what happened to Joseph. God saw that Joseph had been faithful, and He made his dream of destiny a reality. Notice that in Genesis 41:14 it says, "They brought him quickly out of the dungeon." One morning Joseph woke up in the dungeon—and the next day he woke up in the palace. One morning Joseph woke up as a prisoner—and the next day he arose as the second most powerful man in the world! The Power Test comes very, very suddenly.

Where Does Power Come From?

Psalm 62:11 tells us where power comes from: "God has spoken once, twice I have heard this: that power belongs to God." This verse says that power "belongs to God"—so if we have power, it has come from God. God is the One who gives us power.

One of my favorite Scripture passages is in John 19—Pilate is talking to Jesus about power. Pilate doesn't seem to realize where his power comes from.

> Then Pilate said to Him, "Are You not speaking to me? Do You not know that I have power to crucify You, and power to release You?" Jesus answered, "You could have no power at all against Me unless it had been given you from above" (John 19:10-11).

I think this is one of the most humorous passages in the Bible—because Pilate is actually talking to God and saying, "Don't you realize that I have power over you?" Pilate just didn't understand, did he?

Jesus straightened him out when he said, "You could have no power at all against Me unless it had been given you from above." Jesus let Pilate know that all power and all authority come from above—from

God Himself.

And God has given every person power in some area of his or her life, and every person is a leader to some degree. What kind of a leader are you? Are you a humble leader? Are you a servant-leader? What are you doing with the power God has given you? God is looking for good stewards whom He can trust with His power. He wants us to recognize that power comes from Him. And He wants us to walk in humility.

How Do We Receive Power?

It is very simple. As with everything else in the Bible, if you want to have power, you do just the opposite of what you think you're supposed to do! I don't know if you've noticed this yet, but in the kingdom of God everything is opposite. This has been called the spiritual law of paradox.

If you want to have authority, then you must be under authority (see Mark 9:35).

If you want to truly live, you must first die (see Matt. 16:25).

If you want to receive, give (see Luke 6:38).

With God, it is all opposite of the world's ways. So in order to get power, you must *give up the right to power*. You must become a servant.

James 4:10 says: "Humble yourselves in the sight of the Lord, and He will lift you up." We already know that power comes from God. So it is God who lifts us up, or gives us power. And this verse is telling us that if we want God to lift us up, or give us power, we must *humble ourselves* in His sight.

First Peter 5:5-6 tells us how to do that.

Likewise you younger people, submit yourselves to your elders. Yes, all of you be submissive to one another, and be clothed with humility, for "God resists the proud, but gives grace to the humble." Therefore humble yourselves under the mighty hand of God, that He may exalt you in due time.

Again, the Bible is telling us that the way to promotion is to humble ourselves. God's Word tells us to "be submissive . . . and be clothed with humility" (v. 5). To our natural minds that may sound like the least likely way to get power—but remember, in the kingdom of God everything is opposite. God says that if we do these things, then He will "exalt [us] in due time" (v. 6). In other words, God will give us authority, responsibility and influence when we pass the test.

Notice that 1 Peter 5:5 also says that "God resists the proud." I want to tell you something very important: To have the Creator of the universe resisting you is *not* a good thing! To help illustrate this truth, I'm going to compare the Christian life to a game of football.

I think football is a fun game; and in much the same way, I think the Christian life is a fun way of life. In fact, I think the Christian life is the most fun way of life there is—and one reason it is so much fun is that God lets us "run with the ball." God doesn't make all the touchdowns. In fact, He wants *us* to make the touchdowns! God hands us the ball, and then He says, "Here, you can teach. Here, you can pray for the sick. Here, you can lead someone to Jesus. Here, you can be a group leader at church. Here, you lead. You can do this!" Then He adds, "The only thing I ask you to do is to just *stay behind Me*. If you just stay behind Me, I'll take care of all the obstacles."

In the beginning, it's easy for us to stay behind God. The first time we're asked to lead in some kind of ministry situation, we know we can't do it on our own. We say, "I don't think I can do this. I'm not a leader, God." That is when God says, "You don't have to be a leader. You just have to follow. Follow Me."

At first we follow very closely behind Him. We want to stay extremely close to God, because we know that without Him we can't do anything. Then, after we finish that first assignment, everyone cheers—especially if we have made a touchdown. Everyone comes up to us afterward and says, "Man, you're really good at this!"

That feels pretty good—so the next time that God says, "Here, take the ball again," we're a little more confident. When God hands us the ball, we say, "OK! OK! I've got it, Lord!" And this time we might even step out and dodge a little bit, showing off a few moves. Pretty soon, everything is going great. Before we know it, we've become used to the fact that God is out in front of us doing the work.

Then a time comes when God hands us the ball, but we say, "You know, God, I don't think I need to stay behind You anymore. I think I've got this figured out now. I can do this myself now, Lord. You can go and sit down, because I've got this covered."

Let me tell you something: *God does not sit down!* The Bible says God "resists the proud" (1 Pet. 5:5). And when we walk in pride, this is what happens:

God hands us the ball and says, "Just stay behind Me."

We say, "Not necessary anymore. I don't need You, God."

God says, "What?"

We say, "I think I can do this by myself." And then we step out from behind God, and we try to move forward on our own.

"OK," God says, but then He steps in front of us, turns and faces us, and assumes a tackling position—and God is one *big* linebacker, if you know what I mean!

Then God says, "C'mon—let's see how far you can get now."

That is what happens when we walk in pride. The Bible makes it very clear that God opposes us, resists us and blocks our moves when we walk in pride.

Joseph was a prime candidate for pride. We know from what we've read so far that he was handsome, intelligent and had great ability. He was the favorite son, although he had 10 older brothers. He even had the affirmation and endorsement of God on his life—and yet Joseph walked in humility.

And Pharaoh said to Joseph, "I have had a dream, and there is no one who can interpret it. But I have heard it said of you that you can understand a dream, to interpret it." So Joseph answered Pharaoh, saying, "It is not in me; God will give Pharaoh an answer of peace" (Gen. 41:15-16).

Pharaoh had heard that Joseph could interpret dreams. But Joseph refused to take the credit for that gift. Joseph said, "No, it is not in me to interpret dreams. It is God who will do that." Joseph understood that he needed to stay behind God. That is the humility that Joseph walked in. And because of Joseph's humility, God was able to trust him with His power.

Humility is attractive and pride is always ugly! Have you ever noticed that? Think about it for a moment. Have you ever met someone who was very successful but also very prideful? Are you attracted to that person? No, because pride is repulsive! No matter how successful a person might be, pride has a way of making him or her very unattractive. But what if you meet someone who is very successful and also very humble? That is very attractive!

> *No matter how successful a person might be, pride has a way of making him or her very unattractive.*

I must admit there is one thing that I really don't understand: someone who has never been successful at all, and yet still manages to be prideful. Now that is just downright silly! Pride always looks foolish— and to illustrate my point, I'm going to tell on me!

About 20 years ago, someone gave me a really nice pair of shoes. I didn't have any nice clothes at that time. We didn't have much back then in the way of material things, and an acquaintance had bought some really expensive shoes for me. They were lizard-skin shoes; and whenever I walked in them, I just felt like the king of the jungle. I would think, *Everyone probably thinks that I'm rich when they see me in these shoes. When I walk into a room with these shoes on, people just can't help but notice me.* Believe me, I thought those shoes said wonderful things about who I was!

Then one Saturday I went to a car wash, and the place was packed with people. I went inside to wait, and I discovered there was a place where you could get your shoes shined. I thought to myself, *I'm going to get my shoes shined, so everyone here can see how important I am. Hopefully they didn't see me get out of that Ford Fairlane. Hopefully, when they see these shoes, they will think that Mercedes out there is mine.*

So I got my shoes shined, stepped down and began to walk down the long glass walkway where people stand to watch their cars being washed. Everyone was standing at the glass, so I walked very slowly, taking my time in my nice, shiny lizard-skin shoes. As I passed, everyone would turn slightly; and when they turned, I noticed that their eyes would get big. Everyone was glancing down at my feet. *Wow*, I thought, *This is great! These shoes are real attention-getters!*

I was just loving it. So I got down to the end of that walkway and thought to myself, *I'm just going to glance down and see how nice those shoes look.* When I looked down, I could see that the guy who shined my shoes had turned my pant-legs up—and had forgotten to turn them back down after he finished. People were staring all right—but not at my fancy shoes!

Pride always looks foolish, doesn't it? But humility is attractive. And when we walk in humility, God will lift us up. When we walk in humility, God will give us power.

All power comes from God—and we get it by being humble. We get it by giving up the right to power and becoming servants instead.

What Is the Purpose of Power?

The Bible tells us that God gave power to Jesus when Jesus walked this earth. Acts 10:38 says: "God anointed Jesus of Nazareth with the Holy Spirit and with power, [He] went about doing good and healing all who were oppressed by the devil, for God was with Him."

God gave Jesus power. And what did Jesus do with that power? He went about doing good deeds. God gave Jesus power so that He could do good—so that He could heal people and set people free from the oppression of the devil. God gives power to each of us so that we can help other people.

God did not give power to Joseph for Joseph's sake. God gave power to Joseph so that Joseph could feed the world during a severe famine! God looked down and said, "There are seven years of famine coming. I need someone I can trust to take care of these people for Me during the famine. Otherwise a lot of people are going to die." In Joseph, God found a man who would be humble, who would be faithful and who would be a good steward—a man He could trust to feed the nations.

God's heart is always for people—so God's power is always given to help people. That is what power is for, and God wants us to remember that.

In Deuteronomy 8, the Lord lets the Israelites know He is going to help them enter the Promised Land, and that they will possess many good things there through His power. He tells them not to forget about that after they have entered the land; and He reminds them that power comes from Him.

Finally, He warns them against saying in their hearts, "'My power and the might of my hand have gained me this wealth.' And you shall remember the LORD your God, for it is He who gives you power to get wealth, that He may establish His covenant which He swore to your fathers, as it is this day" (Deut. 8:17-18). God wants His people to remember that power comes from Him, not from their own efforts. And God says that the purpose of power is so He may "establish His covenant." The purpose of wealth is that He may "establish His covenant." The purpose of influence is that God may "establish His covenant."

God wants to establish His covenant in this earth—and His covenant is a covenant of blessing. His covenant is a covenant of healing. His covenant is a covenant of deliverance from sin and darkness!

Recently God gave our church body a piece of property in a highly visible location on a major highway. God did that because He wants to *establish His covenant* with the people in that area. God looked down and saw 40,000 cars driving by that property every day—and most of those cars were being driven by people who are destined for hell unless someone tells them about Jesus Christ. That is why God gave our church that property—and that is the reason God gives us influence on this earth.

At our church, we have determined that we are going to keep on serving people, whatever our level of influence might be. We are going to keep on doing the same things that we started out doing when our church was smaller: loving people, helping people, seeing marriages restored and sending missionaries around the world. The more God increases our influence, the more we are going to be about the business of His kingdom!

I see this principle modeled all the time at the church I pastor. Now I realize that I am somewhat biased, but I honestly believe that some of the world's greatest servants are in our church. They are willing to stay late, come in at odd times and basically just lay down their lives in order to serve others. And they truly care for one another, as Paul exhorted us to do: "Let each of you look out not only for his own interests, but also for the interests of others" (Phil. 2:4).

I see this illustrated beautifully at those times when God uses one of our pastors to speak a prophetic word of encouragement for someone in the congregation. I look out over the congregation, and I see the Spirit of God ministering to that person—and that blesses me. Then I notice that the people nearby are just as happy and excited as the person who is being ministered to—and that blesses me even more. People are happy because God is blessing their brother or sister in the Lord, and that is the right attitude!

As a pastor, I just love to see such love demonstrated—and I believe God likes it, too! Why? Because God's heart is about people. He likes to see His children serving one another and ministering to one another. That is why He gives us power and ministry gifts, particularly the prophetic ministry.

And every time God promotes us or gives us a position of influence, it is because He has *people* in mind. He has someone in mind—someone He wants us to minister to.

One day, a lady in our church was driving her daughter to school, and her heart was breaking for her little girl. Her husband had recently abandoned the family, leaving her and the children to fend for themselves. And now it was "Father-Daughter Day" at school.

Yet when this mother pulled up to the school, she was surprised to see Pastor Jeff Drott (one of the pastors at our church) standing there at the curb. The little girl ran up to Pastor Jeff and hugged him, her day obviously brightened by this unexpected surprise. Then she said, "Pastor

Jeff, what are you doing here?"

"I'm going to be your daddy today," he replied. The biggest smile you have ever seen appeared on that little girl's face; and off they walked, hand in hand. She would have a "daddy" at school with her that day just like the other little girls!

That is what influence is for. That is what power is for. God gives us power and influence because *He loves people desperately*. He wants us to use His power to reach them with His love.

Power is not a bad thing, it is a good thing—and it comes from God. It comes for the purpose of helping others. You may not even know how much influence you have, but you do have influence. And God is watching to see if you will handle your power wisely, to see if you will use it to do His work. He is watching to see if you will use your influence and authority to share His love with a lost and dying world. That is the Power Test. Will you pass it?

CHAPTER EIGHT

THE PROSPERITY TEST

As we discovered in the previous chapter, power will test your character. But so will money. In fact, money is really just another form of power. Money can give us the power to do certain things; and in the same way, the lack of money can hinder us from doing certain things. Thus money empowers us to some extent.

The Prosperity Test: Using Money Wisely

The question is, What do we do with the power that our money brings us? Do we use it as God would have us use it—to further His purposes for our lives and the lives of others? Or do we squander it in foolish ways—or worse yet, in ways that are actually harmful?

This is the Prosperity Test, and every one of us has taken it. We will take this test as long as we are living on this earth because while we're here, we need material things in order to survive. We need food, we need shelter, and we need clothing. And money is just something that we use to exchange for those things we need.

If you think you're too spiritual to bother with material things, try going without food and clothing for a while. You'll quickly discover that while money cannot provide happiness or contentment, the lack of it can certainly create problems!

This is why God is so interested in the way that we handle our money. Our money is a medium that God Himself uses in order to further His purposes on this earth. God wants to see people fed and clothed and provided for. And He uses *people* to distribute His resources. He uses *people* to distribute money and take care of needs on this earth. So it is only natural that He looks for those who know how to manage money wisely, according to His principles.

He found such a person in Joseph.

In Genesis 41:2-7, we find the account of Pharaoh's perplexing dreams. First Pharaoh dreamed he saw seven fat cows and seven thin cows; and the seven thin cows ate the seven fat cows. Then Pharaoh dreamed that he saw seven plump stalks of grain and seven thin and blighted stalks of grain; and the seven thin stalks ate the seven plump stalks. The Bible tells us that Pharaoh's spirit was troubled about these dreams (see Gen. 41:8). Somehow, Pharaoh knew that these dreams were significant!

So he searched desperately to find someone who could tell him the meaning of the dreams. This is how Joseph came to be called out of the prison and stand before Pharaoh. Let's pick up the story in verse 25.

> Then Joseph said to Pharaoh, "The dreams of Pharaoh are one; God has shown Pharaoh what He is about to do: The seven good cows are seven years, and the seven good heads are seven years; the dreams are one. And the seven thin and ugly cows which came up after them are seven years, and the seven empty heads blighted by the east wind are seven years of famine. This is the thing which I have spoken to Pharaoh. God has shown Pharaoh what He is about to do. Indeed seven years of great plenty will come throughout all the land of Egypt; but after them seven years of famine will arise, and all the plenty will be forgotten in the land of Egypt; and the famine will deplete the land. So the

plenty will not be known in the land because of the famine following, for it will be very severe. And the dream was repeated to
Pharaoh twice because the thing is established by God, and God
will shortly bring it to pass" (Gen. 41:25-32).

Two times Joseph said, "God has shown Pharaoh what He is about
to do" (v. 25,28). God had a purpose in showing Pharaoh those dreams—
a purpose of blessing, provision and deliverance from starvation! God
knew that seven years of famine were coming, and He wanted to make
sure that people didn't starve. So He showed Pharaoh what was about to
happen.

But there was more that God was trying to do. God had a plan to
provide food for everyone during the famine—and He had to have someone whom He could trust to carry out His plan. He had to have someone
who would obey Him in the area of money. And He found that person
in Joseph. Joseph understood God's principles about managing
finances—and like the faithful servant that he was, Joseph offered that
wisdom to Pharaoh.

> Now therefore, let Pharaoh select a discerning and wise man,
> and set him over the land of Egypt. Let Pharaoh do this, and let
> him appoint officers over the land, to collect one-fifth of the
> produce of the land of Egypt in the seven plentiful years. And let
> them gather all the food of those good years that are coming,
> and store up grain under the authority of Pharaoh, and let them
> keep food in the cities. Then that food shall be as a reserve for
> the land for the seven years of famine which shall be in the land
> of Egypt, that the land may not perish during the famine (Gen.
> 41:33-36).

God had a plan to make sure that there would be plenty of food for
everyone when the years of famine came. But His plan would have failed
in the hands of someone who did not know how to manage money wisely. God couldn't choose someone who wouldn't let Him be first in their
decisions and whose checkbook was in disarray. He couldn't choose

someone with a pattern of unrestrained spending, who didn't know how to save up or to wait. If He had chosen someone like that, the grain would have been gone before the famine arrived! God looked for someone who was a good steward, someone who knew how to manage material things according to His principles. The Prosperity Test was a huge part of Joseph's destiny. Would he manage the wealth of those years of plenty as God wanted him to?

The Prosperity Test will be a huge part of your destiny as well. Until you are found faithful in the area of money, you will not be able to step into your destiny to the full extent that God desires—because God's plans for you will always involve bringing His blessings and provision to others.

Like it or not, it takes money to do that! It takes money to meet the needs of hurting people and carry the gospel around the world—and it takes money to support your family while you are doing that! God will give you everything you need to carry out His plans for your life. Can He trust you to handle it wisely? Or will you squander what He gives you by foolish spending? This is the Prosperity Test.

You might be saying to yourself, *I never have any money. I always seem to be broke. How could I be taking the Prosperity Test?* The truth is, everyone has financial resources to manage. Every time you get your paycheck, you are taking the Prosperity Test. Every time that you get any extra money, you are taking the Prosperity Test. Even if you are living on welfare, you will take the Prosperity Test each time you get that check from the government. (Remember that Jesus took note of how people gave offerings in the Temple, including the widow with only two mites to her name [see Mark 12:41-44].)

It's unavoidable. We will all be tested in how we handle our money. And it seems that here in the United States we have a lot more money to be tested by!

You Take the Prosperity Test *Every Day*

I know you've probably heard this before, but it is worth repeating: The United States is the most prosperous nation in the world. People in

America have more materially than four out of every five people on this earth. So if you live in the United States, you take the Prosperity Test every day.

Let me give you some statistics to help you see what I mean. According to the World Bank, the average household income of someone living in the United States in the year 2002 was $35,400. Now let's compare that figure with the average household income for people living in other countries of the world that same year:

Japan	$34,010
Finland	$23,890
Israel	$16,020
Saudi Arabia	$8,530
Mexico	$5,920
Argentina	$4,220
Turkey	$2,490
Russia	$2,130
China	$960
India	$470
Nigeria	$300

Source: World Bank; GNI Per Capita in US$, Atlas Method

Those figures show the difference between the income that the rest of the world lives on and the average income that we live on here in the United States. When we look at those numbers, it helps us understand that we in the United States enjoy a greater degree of material prosperity than nearly everyone else on this planet.

Here in America, we are so prosperous that we pray for things the rest of the world would never dream of praying for. We pray for things like new clothes or a bigger home. While the rest of the world is praying for a bicycle for transportation or food to put on the table, we pray for a better car than the one we are already driving.

A friend of mine is now involved in full-time missions work; but when he first began traveling as a missionary, he didn't have much experience with the economic differences between our country and most other countries. This became painfully obvious on one occasion when he was preaching a message on suffering—he made the mistake of using an illustration that he had developed here in America. The example that he used was taken from a year in his life when he and his wife had to get by with only one car.

That was his example of suffering! And yet he was preaching that message in a country in which 96 percent of the people did not even own one car! He was preaching in a country whose average citizen earned about $2,000 a year!

Unfortunately, many of us have absolutely no comprehension of how the rest of the world lives. Here in America we live in a prosperity bubble, and we have no idea how richly blessed and prosperous we really are. We are living the Prosperity Test every day. Whether we realize it or not, we have been entrusted with great material wealth.

The critical question is, What are we going to do with that wealth?

In the same way that power tests the true character of every person, money tests it too. Every time you get your paycheck, you have a test handed to you.

Unexpected income is a particularly revealing test. Have you ever had a windfall—perhaps a raise or a surprise bonus at the end of the year? When you did, you took the Prosperity Test! It doesn't matter whether it was a $10,000 raise, a $1 per hour raise, a $1,000 bonus or a $50 bill. Any time you receive additional funds, you take the Prosperity Test. Because every time you receive extra money, you have a chance to tell God how well you're going to manage the income He gives you.

What did you do with that extra money? Did you save it, did you spend it, did you blow it, did you pay down your debt?

It is amazing how we pray and ask God for extra money—but then when it comes into our hands, we're not faithful to do what God would want us to do with it. Why would God continue to give us extra funds if we're not faithful with the funds that He does give us? Let's think about that—and realize that every time we receive any additional funds we will take the Prosperity Test.

Every person will be tested by money, whether he or she has only a little or a lot. That's why Jesus said, "Where your treasure is, there your heart will be also" (Matt. 6:21). In other words, Jesus says your *money* will always be tied to your *heart*.

Does money control you—or do you control money?

And God is very interested in our hearts. The Bible says: "For the LORD does not see as man sees; for man looks at the outward appearance, but the LORD looks at the heart" (1 Sam. 16:7). God is looking at our *hearts* to see if they truly belong to Him. And Jesus said the way we handle our money is a primary indicator of where our hearts really belong.

So it is very important to settle this question: What has first place in your heart? Is it God? Or is it money? Does money control you—or do you control money?

Let God Be First

The most important principle I can tell you about money can be summed up in four simple words: *Let God be first!*

You let God be first in your life by *honoring* Him above all else. The Bible tells us, "Honor the LORD with your possessions, and with the firstfruits of all your increase" (Prov. 3:9). Do you honor God with the firstfruits of your finances?

Finances are just one way that we can show honor to God and let Him know He is first in our lives. Joseph honored God and let Him be first in everything that he had. Joseph even honored God in the naming of his children. In the midst of the seven years of plenty, Joseph had two sons. Genesis 41 tells the story.

And to Joseph were born two sons before the years of famine came, whom Asenath, the daughter of Poti-Pherah priest of On, bore to him. Joseph called the name of the firstborn Manasseh: "For God has made me forget all my toil and all my father's house." And the name of the second he called Ephraim: "For God has caused me to be fruitful in the land of my affliction" (vv. 50-52).

The name Manasseh means "to forget," and the name Ephraim means "to be fruitful." But the first thing that Joseph had to say about the names of his children was "for God"! "*For God* has made me forget. . . . *For God* has caused me to be fruitful" (emphasis added). Joseph recognized that it was God who had made him forget his troubles and it was God who had made him fruitful. So Joseph gave God the honor for it. Joseph had stepped into a place of incredible power and wealth—but in that place of privilege and comfort, he did not forget God. As the ruler of all Egypt, Joseph was still thanking God and honoring Him. His two sons were the firstfruits of his body—and Joseph chose to *honor God* with those firstfruits! He used their names as a means to give honor to God for all that God had done for him. It was an outward reflection of the gratitude in his heart.

This is really what tithing is about—giving God the *honor* and the thanks for everything that we have. You may have heard about tithing many times over the years. Or you may be hearing about it for the first time. Nevertheless, tithing is really very simple. It is about *putting God first*.

God has always been interested in knowing what is *first* place in our hearts. That is why God has always been interested in the *firstfruits* and the *firstborn*. He wants to see what is *first* in our hearts.

Why did God accept Abel's offering, but not Cain's? Because Abel's offering was the *firstborn*! But Cain's offering was *not* the firstfruits—so his offering was not blessed (see Gen. 4:3-5).

When the Israelites first entered the Promised Land, God commanded them to give all the silver and the gold from Jericho to Him (see Josh. 6:19). Why? Because Jericho was the *first* city they conquered—so

Jericho was the *firstfruits* of the Promised Land! Notice that God didn't tell them to first take 10 cities and then give one of those cities to Him when it was all over. No, God commanded them to give everything from that *first* city to Him—and after they did that, He said that they could have the goods from all the other cities.

This is how the principle of the firstfruits works in our lives: Giving the *first* to God causes the rest to be blessed. God told the Israelites that if they would just *honor Him* with that first city, then He would help them conquer all the other cities. Further, He would allow them to keep everything from all the other cities. But when Achan kept part of the silver from Jericho for himself, the Israelites found that God was no longer helping them. Instead of having God's help, they were on their own—and the battle did not go well for them! Until they made that "dishonoring" situation right with God, they were not able to go on and capture any more cities (see Josh. 7).

The tithe is blessed and consecrated to God before you take it—but if you take it, it is cursed!

The tithe is always the *first* part, not the last. God said that when the Israelites' sheep had a lamb, they were to give the *first* lamb to Him. God did not say to let the sheep have 10 lambs, and then give 1 of the 10 to Him. God said to give Him the *first* one. Why? *Because it takes faith to give the first one!* It takes faith to give the *first* 10 percent, not the last 10 percent! Tithing is 10 percent, and it does mean a tenth part—but tithing is about giving the *first* tenth to God!

Giving the last 10 percent instead of the first 10 percent is saying, "Once I am sure that I am taken care of, I will take care of You, God. If I have enough room in my life for You, I will honor and obey You." That is not really very honoring to God, is it? But when we give God the *first* 10 percent, we are taking a step of faith and trust. We are saying, "God, I want to take care of You first. You are first place in every area of my life, God."

You can *claim* God is first place in your life—but let me see your check register! By observing where your money goes, I can tell you who is *really* first place in your life. It could be the mortgage company; it could be the electric company. I'll tell you who is first place in a lot of people's lives. Can you guess? It's Visa!

But let me tell you who ought to be first—God!

When God is first in our lives, He blesses the rest. This is a principle we see throughout the Bible. So put God first! The first check I write every month is the tithe check. Not the second check or the third check or the eighth check—the *first* check. Because I want to give God the *first* part of all my increase, not the last part!

In May 2003, Barna Research Group released the results of a study about tithing. The study showed that the proportion of households in the United States that tithe their income to the church has dropped from 8 percent in 2001 to just 3 percent in 2002. So according to this respected research organization, only 3 percent of households in the United States tithe.[1] Yet we are the most prosperous nation on Earth!

God has blessed this nation because we have sent missionaries all around the world to spread His gospel message. I believe America has been living in years of prosperity and years of the blessings of God. But I also believe that years of famine are right around the corner if we do not start honoring Him with the firstfruits of those blessings.

We have been blessed because of God. And if we turn our backs on Him, we are going to be in trouble! So let's make a commitment to make God first!

How can you do your part? Any time that you get some unexpected money, you have a great opportunity to let God be first. When you get a bonus or some unexpected money, do you tithe on it? Do you honor God first? Tithing is simply a way of expressing your gratitude to God. Tithing is a way of acknowledging that He is the One who got you that raise or that bonus in the first place.

Imagine the message it sends when someone prays, "God, please, God, please! We need extra money!" Then, when God answers that prayer by sending the extra money, they don't even tithe on it!

Isn't it amazing how quickly we forget that it was God who met that need and sent us the money? When we tithe, we are letting God know that we are grateful for that money and that we realize it came from Him. But if we immediately forget God and don't honor Him with the tithe on that money, we are not letting God be first.

Please understand me. This is not law—this is *love!* This is expressing love and gratitude and honor to the God who has given us everything!

God is so gracious and so compassionate. When we are in a tight spot, God will say, "OK, I want to bless you. I want to help you. Even though you have some things out of line in your life, I know that you need this money right now. You are My child and I love you. So I'm going to help you. I'm going to put it on your boss's heart to give you a raise, even though no one else in the company is getting a raise right now." God loves you so much that in some cases He will move upon the heart of an unbeliever, just to get you a raise. So be sure to thank Him for it! Be sure to honor Him for all that He does for you.

Let God be first—this is the first principle of the Prosperity Test. There are other financial principles that are important as well, and we need to understand those principles. Joseph understood the importance of these other principles. These principles were essential to his success in his destiny as ruler of the world's food supply during the years of famine.

Of course, Joseph understood the most important principle—He allowed God to be first in every area of his life. But Joseph also understood the importance of something else that we would all do well to comprehend—*learning to wait.*

Good Things Come

For those seven years of abundance, Joseph made the Egyptians store up, store up and store up. After a while, I'm sure some of the people probably said, "We've got enough grain stored up by now! Why can't we just use some of this grain, instead of storing it up?" And Joseph most likely replied, "No, you don't understand. If you don't store it up now, you're not going to have it later, when you need it."

Joseph understood the importance of waiting. The Egyptians could have used all that extra grain right away, or they could have sold it and made themselves rich overnight. But they would have starved later on, during the famine.

Did you know that the Bible says it is not a good thing to try to get rich quickly? Proverbs 28:20 says, "A faithful man will abound with blessings, but he who hastens to be rich will not go unpunished." So according to the Bible, the get-rich-quick schemes of today are bad for you; and if you get involved in them, you'll be punished! In other words, if you try to get rich quick, you can expect to encounter problems!

Please understand this simple fact: If it sounds too good to be true, it probably is! The Bible warns us over and over again to stay away from get-rich-quick schemes—so just decide right now not to get involved in them.

It is amazing to me how many people get involved in those gimmicks. It is even more amazing to me that Christian people get involved in them! Some Christian people actually want me to get involved in these enterprises—and the reason they want me to get involved is because they see the gift of God on my life. They think they can somehow make themselves rich by using that gift—a gift that God has given to me so that I can help other people and bring them to Him.

I have made a firm decision that I am not going to get involved in anyone's multilevel business. The people in my church know better than to come to me with any get-rich-quick schemes. Many of these ventures appear legitimate; but if you look closely, you will see that they never actually work. They may work for the people who are right at the top. But the reason they work is because of gullible people—and those people are usually right at the bottom! I am saddened to note that nearly every multilevel enterprise goes after the church as a business target. They do that because the tightly knit community that exists within the church makes it a tempting prospecting field.

The church is an organization made up of people, so it is easy to make friends and say, "This is a Christian business that I am involved in." When I hear that statement, I always have a question in my mind: "When did that *business* repent and get saved?" There is no such thing as a Christian business! There are *Christians* and there are *businesses*—and there are Christians who are in business. But a business can't go to heaven or hell! (On second thought, I suppose some of you might think you had a business that *did* go to hell! But enough about that!) Only a *person* can go to heaven or hell. Only a *person* can be a Christian.

Watch out for shortcuts to wealth, because it seems that church folks are a favorite target. Your best safeguard—and this should be no surprise—is God's Word.

In fact, when it comes to wealth, the Bible teaches us *to wait*. The Bible teaches us to *be faithful* and to *be good stewards*. The reason people try to get rich quickly is that they are not willing to live as they ought to financially. They do not want to wait or be patient. They want to have what they want and have it now! They should be learning to save money and to live below their means, but they don't like that idea, so they turn to some shortcut.

We must learn to wait! We need to learn to be patient when it comes to purchases. We should walk away from a possible purchase and think it over for a while. We should look at our budget and ask God if this is His will at the moment. We live in a society of instant gratification—and it is all too easy to fall into the pattern of buying whatever we want at the moment, without being patient or seeking God's counsel about it.

Pride can lead to financial problems if it is not recognized and dealt with.

Not long ago I preached a series on marriage, and in that series I shared something that I believe is important for married couples to understand if they are going to pass the Prosperity Test. Husbands and wives must realize that they sometimes put pressure on each other to buy things that they really cannot afford. Wives put pressure on their husbands and husbands put pressure on their wives for things that simply are unwise for them to have at that point in their lives.

Sometimes the reason is just greed or selfishness—but often the reason is pride. They want to have the expensive things that other couples have, and they feel a need to keep up with the Joneses.

As I said, that is really just pride. And it can lead to financial problems if it is not recognized and dealt with.

Can You Afford It?

But there is a very simple way to defuse that type of conflict. You can prevent pressure from dominating your financial decisions if you just have a budget.

Joseph understood God's principles of financial management—and Joseph had a budget! Joseph said,

> Let [the Pharaoh] appoint officers over the land, to collect one-fifth of the produce of the land of Egypt in the seven plentiful years. And let them gather all the food of those good years that are coming, and store up grain under the authority of Pharaoh (Gen. 41:34-35).

Joseph didn't just vaguely say, "Well, I think it would be a good idea for us to save some of the grain during the years of plenty. Yes, maybe we should think about doing that." No, Joseph had a *plan* in advance, and that plan involved very *specific* amounts—one-fifth to be exact. Joseph's plan also involved *accountability* using Pharaoh's officers. Likewise, a budget will help you to define *specific limits* for your spending, and a budget will also help to keep you and your spouse *accountable* to those limits.

It is hard to say no to your spouse when he or she wants something— I understand that. But you can both keep emotions out of your financial discussions if you simply make a budget and stick to it. Your spouse may come to you and say, "Can we buy a bigger house? Can I buy a new car? Can I have this or have that?" And there is a correct and peaceful answer that goes like this: "I would love to see you have that—but let's see what the budget says."

Then you look at the budget and say, "Oh. I'm sorry. I guess Mr. Budget says, 'No.' I would gladly buy it for you, if it fit into the budget. But Mr. Budget says 'No.'" When you let the budget make the decision, you will have a much more peaceful discussion—and a much less stressful financial life!

Without a budget, it is very difficult to know where your money is going, or even how much money is coming in and going out. So if you don't have a budget, you are not going to be able to succeed financially. You are not going to be able to plan financially either.

I've had people ask me, "Do you think we should buy this new house?" Before they ask me that, they need to understand that the decision to buy a house is not a matter of thinking. It is not a matter of feeling. It is a matter of numbers! Usually it is not really my advice they want, but rather my blessing or endorsement of their decision. But I will not even offer an opinion until I have asked at least one very important question: *"Can you afford it?"*

And all too often the answer I get back goes something like this: "Well—we *feel* like we can."

You can't make your mortgage payment with feelings. It takes money! Financial management isn't about opinion. It's about math! That is why a budget is so important.

This is the way a budget can work to make that sort of decision quite simple: First you calculate all your expenses and compare them to your income. You set aside your tithe and determine how much you want to give in offerings. Then you subtract your taxes, insurance, bills, food, clothing and so on. Finally you come down to a number that is left for the mortgage—and that number will tell you whether you can buy the house or not. It is that simple. Make a budget!

Change Your Life—Make a Budget!

There are certainly more reasons to make a budget than I can list here, but I want to mention seven reasons that will help you see how valuable a meaningful budget can be. If you implement the principle of budgeting, it will change your life in the following ways:

1. *It helps you see things more clearly and objectively.* A budget puts a number on everything, which helps you see financial issues more clearly and objectively. Questions about finances are reduced to the simple comparison of income versus expenses. This helps you keep emotions out of the picture and differentiate between reality and feelings. Without a budget, many people have no idea what their actual monthly income and expenses are. But if you put all the numbers down on paper, you will see your financial situation very clearly. A budget shows you in black and white what exactly you can and can't afford.

2. *It makes you examine and clarify your values and priorities.* When you look at your income and have to make a decision about how to spend it, that forces you to examine what is really most important to you. How much do you value expensive clothing versus saving or giving? How much do you value driving a certain kind of kind of car versus sending your children to college? Which one is a higher priority? How much do you value letting your children have braces as you drive that five-year-old car versus getting that new one? A budget helps you clarify the answer to that question. A budget helps you see the difference between needs and wants, now versus later and important versus unimportant.

3. *It provides a basis of discussion and agreement.* The most powerful tool you have in marriage is unity, yet few married couples are in unity where their finances are concerned. A budget can help you find a place of unity because it provides an opportunity for listening, talking, praying and hearing each other's hearts. When you are able to talk and pray about your budget, you have a basis for finding a place of agreement about your finances. Agreement is the most powerful tool in marriage, while strife and division are deadly.

4. *It provides a basis for accountability.* Mr. Budget helps keep you from overspending, because he has already decided how the money is going to be spent. Mr. Budget can say no to an

impulse purchase by providing accountability that helps keep your finances on track. When you have already determined not to spend outside of your budget, Mr. Budget will tell you whether you can buy something or not.

5. *It helps you live within your means.* A budget provides clear and impartial numbers—letting you know what your actual income is and what you must to do to live within that income. In this way, a budget helps you to live in a land called Reality rather than the lands called Fantasy or Denial—in other words, to live within your means. Many people live with unnecessary stress because they have foolishly taken on financial obligations that are bigger than their actual income. A budget helps by revealing the lifestyle your income can realistically support. Many people could greatly reduce the stress in their lives if they would simply downsize their lifestyle to fit their income.

6. *It helps you live without debt.* God wired you to benefit from patience. He wired you to enjoy looking forward to things. He wired you for something called hope. Do you know what debt does? It robs you of the opportunity to hope. When you borrow every time you want something, you don't have to hope for it anymore—instead, you just go put it on the credit card. This is why people who are in debt are the most discouraged people in the world. They have no opportunity for delayed gratification, and that robs them of the joy and happiness that come when a hope is fulfilled. If you just pull out the credit card every time something strikes your fancy, you will live in continual discouragement. That discouragement can start a cycle of debt in which you want to buy something every time you feel discouraged. Then the debt increases, which creates more discouragement, and the cycle goes on. Perhaps you know exactly what I am talking about. When you get a little low, you just want to buy something in order to create that short-lived surge of excitement. It's seductively easy to get in the habit of buying things without hope.

7. *It builds character and discipline in your life.* A budget holds up a
set of numbers and asks you to live within them. Will you
stick to the commitment that you made to God and to your
spouse when you prayed and set up that budget? Or will you
go back on your word when the pressure is on, when the
temptation to spend is tugging at you? Sticking to a budget
is like sticking to any other commitment. It takes character.
It takes discipline. And these are vital qualities to have if
you're going to fulfill God's destiny for your life.

I want to emphasize that last statement because it is so important.
*You will never fulfill the spiritual destiny that God has on your life if you cannot
pass the Prosperity Test.* If you can't handle money correctly and according
to biblical principles, how will you be able to handle the other issues that
are important to your destiny?

As with everything else God has given you stewardship over, He is
watching to see if you will handle money wisely and for Him. Having a
budget is a first step toward taking responsibility for your money, and
showing God that you will be faithful with those things He has placed
in your care.

Joseph had a budget. And Joseph developed his budget so well that
after seven years of savings, he fed the entire world during seven years of
famine. Now that is God's style of budgeting! And one way Joseph did it
was by living on less than the amount that was actually coming in—what
I like to call living below your means.

Live Below Your Means

Most people think they understand what it is to live below their means—
but most people really do not. Living on 90 to 95 percent of your income
is not living below your means.

Truly living below your means actually requires living on about 70
percent of your income. Just add it up and you will see what I mean: If
you tithe 10 percent, put 10 percent in savings, put 10 percent in retire-
ment or other investments, and give something in offerings above your

tithes, you're going to be living on 60 to 70 percent of your income at the highest level. Yet rather than living below their means, many people are living above them.

Many people do not have the income to support the lifestyle they are leading—and the reason they are living that way is pride. They want to drive the same type of cars their friends are driving, and they want to live in the same type of homes or apartments that their friends are living in. But they do not make enough income right now to do that, so they get themselves into all kinds of financial difficulties.

God never intended our financial decisions to be dictated by what other people are driving or wearing. In fact, God tells us quite clearly the approach that He wants us to have toward our money and our lifestyle.

> Now godliness with contentment is great gain. For we brought nothing into this world, and it is certain we can carry nothing out. And having food and clothing, with these we shall be content. But those who desire to be rich fall into temptation and a snare, and into many foolish and harmful lusts which drown men in destruction and perdition. For the love of money is a root of all kinds of evil, for which some have strayed from the faith in their greediness, and pierced themselves through with many sorrows (1 Tim. 6:6-10).

God says that if we have food and clothing, we are to be content. He does not say that we are to be content with these things if we live in India or Africa or Haiti. The Bible doesn't put forth a different standard for those of us who live in the United States. No, He simply says that believers are to *be content* with those things. This is not a cultural issue—this is the Bible! As long as we have food and clothing, we are to be content!

But the love of money and the desire to be rich will tell you that you should not be content with mere food and clothing. Greed will tell you that in order to be content you must have more. It will tell you that you can never be happy unless you buy "this" or have "that." Greed is never satisfied—and that is why this Scripture passage says that those who are greedy "fall into temptation and a snare," and "pierce themselves through with many sorrows."

Ecclesiastes 5:10 says: "He who loves silver will not be satisfied with silver; nor he who loves abundance, with increase."

The love of money is never satisfied. Greed will push you to buy things that you don't really need. Because of this, many Americans put themselves under a burden of debt, and they end up with ulcers and other health problems brought on by financial stress. But God never intended us to live that way! God does not want us to live in debt, continually stressed out about our finances. God wants us to be content. As believers we should walk in more contentment than anyone. We should be content with God's provision. True godliness brings with it contentment.

But greediness will rob you of contentment. Greed will push you to live above your means. When you live above your means, you are making a declaration to God. You are saying, "God, I am not content with Your provision—and I am not content with You. I know You have said there are certain ways You have of doing things—but I am not willing to wait for You to work in my life. I am not willing to wait for the things that I want. I have to have them now! So I am going to figure out a way that I can get more, without You."

Do you think God is going to bless a person like that? When God looks down and sees a selfish, greedy person who is violating His scriptural principles, do you think He says, "I'm just going to give him more?" No. A person like that may end up getting more—but he is getting more by working more, not by the blessings of God.

Make no mistake about it: God *wants* to give us more. He *wants* to bless us and give us the desires of our hearts. But as with everything else, in order to have God's blessings, we must be willing to do things His way and abide by His principles.

It really bothers me when I see believers struggling financially and then blaming God for their situation. Some people even reach a place of such discouragement that they don't believe God wants to bless them. They blame God, as if He is letting them down—and yet the reason they are struggling financially is because they have violated scriptural principles with their unbridled spending.

They are not content as God commanded us to be, so they live above their means. Then they end up borrowing money that they should not be borrowing, just to support that lifestyle. Because of their own poor financial management, they end up in trouble—and then they wonder why God doesn't seem to be blessing them the way that they think He should. They blame God for not coming through. But their financial problems are their own fault, not God's. They have fallen prey to the *deceitfulness* of riches.

Don't Be Deceived

Yes, riches can actually be deceitful. First Timothy 6:9-10 tells us that riches can cause people to fall into a snare and to stray from the faith. Jesus put it this way:

> Now these are the ones sown among thorns; they are the ones who hear the word, and the cares of this world, the deceitfulness of riches, and the desires for other things entering in choke the word, and it becomes unfruitful (Mark 4:18-19).

Jesus says riches have an ability to deceive us. He goes on to say the deceitfulness of riches can even *choke the Word of God* that has been planted in our hearts and make that Word unfruitful. In other words, the deceitfulness of riches can stop the Word of God from producing good fruit in our lives as God intended.

The deceitfulness of riches has even caused some people to stray from their faith! Paul says, "Some have strayed from the faith in their greediness, and pierced themselves through with many sorrows" (1 Tim. 6:10). People have abandoned their families because of money. Some have actually abandoned the Church because of money.

I have known people who have tried attending church and giving—because they think doing so will automatically bring them financial blessing. When that doesn't work for them, they just abandon the church and go somewhere else. They heard someone preaching about the blessings that come from giving and decided to try it, but the motive for their giving had nothing to do with a pursuit of the heart of God. Their motive was to get rich! Do you think God's blessing is going to be poured out on that sort of giving?

God says that if we have food and clothing—in other words, if our basic physical needs are met—we are to be content (see 1 Tim. 6:8). But riches have the ability to deceive us.

I am sad to say that, as a pastor and a minister, I have the opportunity to witness that on a regular basis. For more than 20 years now I have been counseling people about their finances, and I am still shocked to hear about the trouble some believers get themselves into. They come to church every week, and they (supposedly) read the Bible every week. And yet they are not applying the most basic precepts of God's Word to their financial decisions. They are not even applying common sense!

If you think that sounds a bit harsh, let me give you just one example. When we receive requests for financial assistance, quite often it is to help someone make a car payment. Our staff was ministering to a couple that wanted us to make their car payments. So we asked them, "Well, how much are your car payments?"

"One is $600, and the other one is $500," they replied.

"Hmm. That amounts to $1,100 per month just for your car payments then, doesn't it?" we said. "And how much is your income each month?"

"Three thousand, three hundred a month."

"So $1,100 of your $3,300 monthly income is going to car payments?" Please understand—you simply can't do that! I don't know how they came to believe that they could have car payments in that amount on that monthly income, but the numbers simply do not add up. This is not rocket science or even a deep spiritual revelation—this is common sense!

I am shocked at how deeply in debt many young couples are today. And the reason they are under this crushing load of debt is the expensive cars they drive and the pricey apartments (not even the homes!) they rent. They don't really have the income to live that way; but pride, the love of money and the need for instant gratification will not allow them to choose a car or an apartment that fits their financial reality.

I just need to speak the plain truth to some people, though they may not like it.

Whatever happened to driving an affordable, reliable car? Whatever happened to buying a two- or three-year-old car that has already taken the biggest drop in depreciation? Whatever happened to driving an older car back and forth to work, because that is all you do with it—and then having one nice car for other purposes? These are all wisdom principles that we can follow to help us live below our means. Joseph understood these principles, and he utilized them as he saved during the years of plenty!

If you make enough money to drive expensive cars and live in an expensive home, that is fine. But if you don't make that kind of income, don't buy those expensive vehicles and live in those expensive homes. Don't live above your means!

As long as I am giving examples of living above your means, let me share something that I see all too often, and I admit that it bothers me. I see people spending $4 for a cup of coffee—and they have two cups of that pricey coffee every day! Now if you're making $100,000 a year, then you may be able to spend $8 a day on coffee.

If you are living on 60 to 70 percent of your income and have enough extra money to do that, then spend $8 a day on coffee. But if you are living above your means on credit card debt, it is absolutely foolish to spend $4 on a cup of coffee! I don't care how many of your friends are sitting there at that trendy coffee shop! If your budget does not make room for that on a regular basis, then stop going.

I have had younger people be a bit shocked and appalled that I would suggest such a sacrifice. But that is how you live below your means and save up as you invest in your future.

Joseph understood the principles of budgeting and of saving for the future. And because Joseph was such a wise manager of material things, God placed him in charge of the food supply for millions of people. Being faithful in the area of money was essential to Joseph's stepping into his destiny. And it is equally essential for every one of us.

Jesus said that if we are faithful in that which is least, He would set us over much (see Luke 16:10). If we cannot faithfully manage the finances with which God has blessed us, how can we expect to manage the destiny He has promised us?

Luke 16:11 is very clear: "Therefore if you have not been faithful in the unrighteous mammon, who will commit to your trust the true riches?" This really sums up the Prosperity Test. Our destinies are all about handling the true riches of the Kingdom. It seems like Jesus is saying, "If you can't handle money, how will you be able to handle your spiritual destiny?"

It is possible you may be feeling convicted after reading this. I know many people have been living above their means for years, and it has virtually become a lifestyle. If so, I want to ask you to allow the Holy Spirit to work in your heart. Allow the principles that you have just read to change your thinking about finances—and to change the way you are living.

This message can change your life if you take it to heart and decide to do something about it. If you make the decision to live below your means, even if you have to downsize for a season, you will be so grateful 10 years from now.

Because I am a pastor and I love people, my heart is burdened when I see the financial difficulties many of God's people are living with, especially the younger generation. It breaks my heart when I see the places they are living, the vehicles they are driving and the clothes they are wearing, because I know most of them are doing it entirely on debt. They are digging a hole for themselves that may take years to dig out of.

I'm not trying to condemn anyone with this teaching—but I do pray that the conviction of the Holy Spirit will help those in that situation to repent. I pray that they will change their way of living, that they will change their mind about the way they are managing their money— because this is so important to their destinies in God.

Each of us has a spiritual destiny God has planned for our lives. But there are those who will not reach their destinies if they do not get their finances under control. Debt and financial pressure can keep believers in bondage and hold them back from doing the things God has called them to do. Some people have already missed opportunities to do great things for the kingdom of God because of poor financial decisions.

Some have even missed opportunities to have the desires of their heart answered because poor financial management has hindered their path.

But God never intended for us to miss out on realizing our God-given dreams. And God will give us everything we need to fulfill the destiny to which He has called us. The question is: What will we do with the things He has given us?

Let God be first in your finances. Honor Him with the firstfruits of all your increase. Make a budget, live below your means, and learn to wait for the good things that God has promised. When you have been found faithful in handling money, you will pass the Prosperity Test. Then God will be able to promote you, just as He did Joseph, and use you as a channel to distribute His wealth and resources to a hurting and a destitute world.

And reaching a hurting world is the first thing on your Father God's mind when He is dreaming about your destiny. So walk in it!

CHAPTER NINE

THE PARDON TEST

W hat would it be like to be sold as a slave? To narrowly escape being murdered by your own brothers—only to have them sell you into a lifetime of bondage and degradation? As Joseph trudged through the desert to Egypt, hot sand probably stung his eyes, ropes cut through his tender skin, and the cruelty of the traders who had bought him must have seemed small compared to the cruelty and betrayal he had experienced at the hands of his own brothers.

What was going through Joseph's mind as he made that long and painful journey to Egypt? As he stood on an auction block, and was sold to the highest bidder? As he served in the house of Potiphar as a slave? And finally, when he became a husband and a father far from the family he had loved, alone in a pagan land, all because of his brothers' sin and hatred?

Did Joseph have valid reasons to feel betrayed and abused? Most certainly, yes! What had been done to Joseph was not an accident or some sort of misunderstanding. It was treachery.

The Pardon Test: Forgiving Wrongs

The suffering Joseph endured came about because of the deliberate cruelty and malice of others. So Joseph most certainly had reason to be hurt, to be angry and to want justice done. Joseph could have spent those long years consumed with bitterness. He could have spent endless nights going over and over in his mind the horror of what had been done to him. But Joseph did not do that. *Joseph made the decision to forgive.*

How do we know that? The answer is quite simple. We know Joseph made the decision to forgive because we're told "the LORD was with Joseph" (Gen. 39:2). We know Joseph prospered in everything he did (see Gen. 39:3). And that cannot happen if you are holding unforgiveness in your heart. If you are harboring unforgiveness, the presence of God will leave your life. You will simply not be able to move forward into the destiny God has for you.

If Joseph had been walking in unforgiveness, the blessing and presence of God would not have been with him—and that would have kept Joseph from stepping into the destiny God had prepared for him all along.

This is the Pardon Test, and every one of us will have to face this test and pass it. Just like Joseph, every one of us will have to deal with hurtful relationships and wrong, even malicious, behavior. But Joseph passed the Pardon Test with flying colors. Let's read about it.

> When Joseph's brothers saw that their father was dead, they said, "Perhaps Joseph will hate us, and may actually repay us for all the evil which we did to him." So they sent messengers to Joseph, saying, "Before your father died he commanded, saying. 'Thus you shall say to Joseph: "I beg you, please forgive the trespass of your brothers and their sin; for they did evil to you."' Now, please, forgive the trespass of the servants of the God of your father." And Joseph wept when they spoke to him. Then his brothers also went and fell down before his face, and they said, "Behold, we are your servants." Joseph said to them, "Do not be afraid, for am I in the place of God? But as for you, you meant evil against me; but God meant it for good, in order to bring it about as it is this day, to save many people alive. Now therefore, do not be afraid; I will provide for you and your little ones." And he comforted them and spoke kindly to them (Gen. 50:15-21).

This passage gives us the very first appearance of the word "forgive" in the Bible. In Hebrew that word means "absolve" or "release fully." But most of the time that word is not translated "forgive." More often it is translated "bear up" and "lift up."[1]

I find that interesting—because that is exactly what the Lord Jesus Christ did with all of our sins. He *bore* our sins. He *lifted them off* us. When He forgave us of our sins, He took the burden of sin from us and put it on Himself (see Isa. 53:6-12). That is what the word "forgive" really means. It means to take a burden off someone completely and totally. It does not mean to take only part of it off or to just help him or her carry it. It means to lift it off entirely.

The message Joseph's brothers claimed to be bringing from their father asked Joseph to do just that. Their message begged Joseph to *lift off* his brothers the sin they had done against him. Their message asked Joseph to forgive them completely—in other words, to absolve them of guilt and to pardon them.

I really like the word "pardon"—because when you pardon others, you are not holding anything they have done against them anymore. And that is the way God forgives us. When God forgives us, He is not holding our sins against us anymore!

Now think about this: *Is that the way you are forgiving other people?* Are you forgiving them the same way God has forgiven you? Are you releasing them, absolving them and pardoning them—fully and freely, as God does? That is true forgiveness. In order to step into your destiny, you must forgive *the same way God has forgiven you.* Until you do that, you will never fulfill your destiny!

Let me tell you what unforgiveness is like: Holding unforgiveness in your heart is like drinking poison, in the hopes it will hurt the other person. Unforgiveness does not hurt the other person—it hurts you! You are the one who is really going to be hurt when you hold unforgiveness in your heart! Unforgiveness will cause you to live in torment.

Jesus describes this for us in Matthew 18, where He tells the story of the servant who refused to forgive his fellow servant. This is one of the most profound teachings on forgiveness in the Bible, and I encourage you to read the entire passage. Jesus says the master of the unforgiving servant "delivered him to the torturers until he should pay all that was due" (Matt. 18:34).

Jesus said that when you refuse to forgive, you will be tortured or tormented. You will be in bondage until you release that person. The person who hurt you will not be in bondage or torment—you will!

When we hold unforgiveness in our hearts, it hurts us. But it will do more than hurt us and torture us. It will also hinder us from moving forward into our destiny. So if we are going to step into the things God has planned for our lives, we must deal with unforgiveness and leave it behind. We must bury it in the sea of forgetfulness. We must learn to forgive as God has forgiven us.

Keys to Forgiveness: Release, Receive and Believe

I believe the Holy Spirit has shown me some keys about walking in God's forgiveness. In order to forgive as God has forgiven us, we must learn to release, receive and believe.

Release
To forgive others completely is to release them from all charges against them. Even though what they have done is wrong, they are acquitted. They are no longer held guilty for the things they have done. True forgiveness does not continue to look for justice or vindication. True forgiveness releases the wrongdoers from the punishment they deserve.

Remember, this is the way God forgives us! Every one of us has sinned against God, and every one of us has deserved eternal separation from God as a result. But when God forgave our sins, He *released us* from the punishment we deserved. He is no longer holding our sins against us. And that is how He expects us to forgive one another. When we forgive as God forgives, we *release* the person fully.

Joseph made the choice to *release* his brothers and to forgive them completely for everything they had done to him. Joseph took the Pardon Test and passed it with flying colors. He had to make the choice to go on with God or to be consumed with bitterness for the rest of his life—and he chose to move forward with the blessing of God.

Now, let me show you something interesting about this story. After their father, Jacob, died, Joseph's brothers sent messengers to Joseph, saying,

> Before your father died he commanded, saying, "Thus you shall say to Joseph: 'I beg you, please forgive the trespass of your brothers and their sin; for they did evil to you.'" Now, please, forgive the trespass of the servants of the God of your father (Gen. 50:16-17).

I don't know if you've ever noticed this before, but the message Joseph's brothers sent to him was steeped in manipulation! In the first place, Jacob never sent such a message to Joseph. The Bible does not say anything of the sort—it does not even state whether Jacob was ever told the full truth about what had happened to Joseph! What it does state quite clearly is that Joseph's brothers were afraid that Joseph would finally take vengeance on them after their father died. They said to each other, "Father is dead. Maybe Joseph is going to repay us now" (see Gen. 50:15).

I believe these brothers sat around and made this message up word for word. I imagine their discussion going something like this.

> We'll try to get Joseph to believe that our father knew all about it, and that he still wanted Joseph to forgive us for what we did to him. Let's throw in the word "*commanded*"—don't say "ask," that's not strong enough. And don't say, "Jacob commanded." Say, "*Your father*" commanded—that will carry more weight. Oh, and don't just say, "Your brothers." Say, "*The servants of the God of your father.*" Let's get God in on this thing—you know how much Joseph wants to honor God in everything.

I imagine they tried to get the wording exactly right. And for final emphasis, they said, "Before your father died he commanded" (Gen.

50:16). In other words, they wanted Joseph to believe this was the dying wish of his beloved father. Talk about manipulation!

Then their message said, "For they did evil to you" (Gen. 50:17). This was perhaps the most hurtful part of the entire message. Because there was never a "*we* did evil against you." There was never an apology! Joseph's brothers never asked for his forgiveness. They never went to him and said, "*We* did wrong." They phrased it very indirectly, as though it was a message from their father, saying, "*They* did wrong." And instead of going to Joseph themselves, they sent messengers (see Gen. 50:16).

This is what I am trying to show you: Sometimes those who have wronged us will realize it and apologize. Sometimes they will repent and change. But what if they do not? What if they continue to lie and manipulate? What if they never admit they have been wrong? What if they never change their ways? Can you forgive people even when they do not repent? That is a *bigger test*. That is the true test of forgiveness.

You see, it is one thing to forgive someone who has wronged you when that person admits it. When he or she comes to you in brokenness and humility and says, "I'm so sorry. I don't know why I said that. I was tired today, and I said something I didn't mean. Please forgive me."

When someone is truly repentant, it is easy to say, "Yes, I'll forgive you."

But what about the people who refuse to repent? What about the people who continue to lie and manipulate—who walk in pride and won't admit they have done anything wrong? Will you forgive them? Can you forgive them? That is the true test of forgiveness! We must forgive, regardless of whether those who have wronged us ever realize what they have done or repent of it. We must *release* them—and then leave the situation in God's hands.

It is very important to understand this—because if we refuse to forgive, we are putting ourselves in the place of God. God is the only One who has the right to hold something against someone. God is the Judge! You and I are not the judge—God is! And God is the only One who has never wronged anyone.

Joseph understood this truth. That is why he told his brothers, "Do not be afraid, for am I in the place of God?" (Gen. 50:19). Joseph understood that only God had the right to judge his brothers' actions—because *only God is truly just*. God has justified us by the blood of His Son. But He is the only One who is just enough to forgive sin.

The Bible says, "If we confess our sins, He is faithful and just to forgive us our sins and to cleanse us from all unrighteousness" (1 John 1:9). God is just. God is the Judge. He has forgiven us of our sins, and when He cleansed us of our sins, we became sons of the Judge. As sons of the Judge, we are commanded to forgive and to release—but we are not the judge!

Any time you hold unforgiveness against someone, you have set yourself up as judge and jury. You have made yourself the one who determines that person's guilt or punishment. When you do that, you are taking the place of God. When you make yourself the judge, you are leaving God out of it.

If you do not forgive, you will live your life searching for vindication— always trying to prove something rather than trying to please Someone.

But when you forgive that person and release him or her, you release God to act in the situation. You release God to be the Judge He rightfully is. You release God to bring justice on the scene—and God is the only One who can! As hard as you might try to bring justice to a situation, you will never be able to do that—because you are not just! Not one of us is. But God is just—and He is the only one who can bring justice to a situation.

When you forgive someone and release him or her, you also release yourself from torment. You release yourself from the bondage of trying to make that situation right.

If you do not forgive, you will live your life searching for vindication. You will live your life always trying to *prove something* rather than trying to *please Someone*.

There was a time in my life when I was having a hard time forgiving someone. Thoughts about it seemed to flood my mind, no matter where I was. As I was driving down the road, I would be going through an argument in my mind of why he was wrong and I was right. This didn't just happen one time, either. I would go through this in my mind day after day.

Like many Christians, I knew how to play the game. I had actually convinced myself that I had forgiven this man. I would justify my thought patterns in this way: "Of course, I've forgiven him. But one day I will have to talk to him about this. I will need to help him understand the darkness that he walks in." And I actually thought I had forgiven him!

One night I couldn't sleep. It was about two o'clock in the morning, and I had been replaying that obsession over and over in my mind. Have you ever been there? If you have, you know what I'm talking about. You just keep replaying that offense until you can't even go to sleep—and yet you think you've forgiven that person!

Anyway, I was lying there in bed, replaying it over and over in my mind; and suddenly the Lord just broke in on my thoughts. (It's so wonderful when He does that!) The Lord spoke very clearly in my heart and said, "Forgive him!"

"But I have forgiven him," I said.

"No, you have not," the Lord replied. "You are holding this against him. You continue to think about it, and you even talk to other people about it. You have not released him. You have not forgiven him the same way that I have forgiven you—because I am not still thinking about your sin. I am not going around talking to other people about it, either. Now, forgive him!"

"But, God," I said with absolute sincerity, "He was wrong."

"Of course he was wrong," the Lord said to me. "There's no need to forgive people when they are right!"

You don't need to forgive people for being right! I had never thought about it that way before. When you have to forgive people, it is usually not because they have been baking cookies for you, is it? It is because they have been wrong!

God said to me again, "Yes, he was wrong. Now forgive him!"

"But, Lord," I said, "I wasn't wrong in this situation."

I wasn't quite prepared for the Lord's reply. "No, you weren't wrong," He said to me. "But how would you like to have Me bring up some of the situations in which you *were* wrong? *How much time do you have?*"

Ouch! Then the Lord did bring up a situation from my past. It was a situation in which I had been the one who was wrong—and it was not a pleasant remembrance. Then He said to me, "Was what he did to you worse than what you did in that situation?"

"No, Lord," I replied. "What I did back there was much worse than what he did to me."

"That's right," the Lord said. "And I forgave you, didn't I? *Now forgive him.*"

When God said that last "forgive him," I had the distinct feeling that He wasn't just *encouraging* me to forgive—He was *telling* me to! You know, He *is* Lord! He *is* Master! And that means He can *command* us to do it—and we had better just obey!

God told me, "Forgive him and release him."

So I forgave him. That meant I *released* him completely—and I prayed for his good.

I have decided now that I have nothing to prove—but I do have Someone to please. The One I have to please is the Lord Jesus Christ—and I will not be pleasing to Him if I do not forgive! If I hold unforgiveness toward someone, I will always be trying to vindicate myself and to prove that I was right. That is a lonely and miserable way to live.

Joseph could have done that. He could have lived the rest of his life trying to vindicate himself and get justice for the terrible things that had happened to him. Instead, Joseph *released* the situation to God. He went on with his life, and allowed God to vindicate him.

Let me show you a couple of Scripture passages that speak to this issue of releasing those who have wronged you.

> You shall not take vengeance, nor bear any grudge against the children of your people, but you shall love your neighbor as yourself: I am the LORD (Lev. 19:18).

> Dear friends, never avenge yourselves, leave that to God. For it is written, "I will take vengeance, I will repay those who deserve it," says the Lord. Instead, you need to do what the scriptures say, if your enemies are hungry, feed them. If they are thirsty give them something to drink and they will be ashamed of what they have done to you. Don't let evil get the best of you but conquer evil doing good (Rom. 12:19-21, *NLT*).

Perhaps you are more familiar with this translation of Romans 12:19: "'Vengeance is Mine, I will repay,' says the Lord."

God says vengeance belongs strictly to Him. He forbids us to take vengeance for the wrongs that are done to us. We are supposed to leave that up to Him. And the reason we must leave that up to God is because He is the only One who can bring righteous judgment to any situation. That is why vengeance belongs to the Lord.

Receive

I believe the reason many people have a hard time *giving* forgiveness is because *they have never received it.* You can't *give* something to others that you don't *have* yourself. The Bible makes it very clear that there is a connection between our forgiveness of others and God's forgiveness for us.

In the Lord's Prayer, Jesus taught us to pray this way: "And forgive us our debts, as we forgive our debtors. And do not lead us into temptation, but deliver us from the evil one. For Yours is the kingdom and the power and the glory forever. Amen" (Matt. 6:12-13).

I suppose you have prayed the Lord's Prayer at one time or another. When you did, did you realize that you were asking God to forgive you *in the same way that you forgive other people?* (Now that you know that, you might be wishing you hadn't prayed that prayer!)

In the verses immediately following the Lord's Prayer, Jesus explains this further: "For if you forgive men their trespasses, your heavenly Father will also forgive you. But if you do not forgive men their trespasses, neither will your Father forgive your trespasses" (Matt. 6:14-15).

That is an amazing Scripture passage—and I have to admit that I sometimes wish that it was not in the Bible! Jesus Himself said that if we do not forgive others, then He is not going to forgive us. This is what the Bible says—so we had better forgive! And the way that we forgive is in the same way we have been forgiven.

The Lord showed me that one reason people have a difficulty *giving* forgiveness to others is because they haven't really *received* it themselves. There is something inside of us that just seems to have a hard time believing that God has totally and completely forgiven us. And because we haven't *received* His forgiveness ourselves, it is difficult for us to *give* it to others.

Jesus said: "Freely you have received, freely give" (Matt. 10:8).

The only way that you can *freely give* something is if you have *freely received* it. And until you *receive* His forgiveness fully and freely, you won't be able to *give* it fully and freely.

If you believe that you must somehow *earn* your forgiveness, you will make other people earn their forgiveness also. If you believe that somehow you are *paying* for your forgiveness, you will make others pay for forgiveness also.

We fall into this trap all too often. Sometimes we even live as though God Himself is keeping score—after He gave us the best gift He had, His beloved Son, to set us free from the penalty of our sins! We pray as if God is getting back at us for all the stuff we've done wrong! We look at misfortunes in life as God's way of getting even!

If we're a little short in our check register at the end of the month, we might think that God is getting back at us for being late with our tithe. We might even say, "Oh, yes, thank You for getting back at me, Lord. Now we're even. Now we're square. That's good."

Or if we get a flat tire on the way to work, we might think God is getting back at us for our having neglected our morning prayers. We might say, "Yes, thank You, God. I knew You were going to do this, because I didn't have my quiet time this morning. I was supposed to have it, but I got up late. Oh, and now it is starting to rain! That is really a good touch, God. I will really remember this lesson now! Thank You, Lord, for getting back at me. *Now we're even.*"

Can I tell you something very important? *God is never going to get back at you*—because He already "got back" at Jesus! God is never going to get even with you because He already "got even" with Jesus. God is never going to make you pay for the wrong you have done—because Jesus has already paid the penalty in full! Isaiah 53:10 says, "It pleased the LORD to bruise Him." How could it have pleased God to bruise His own Son? It pleased Him because all of our sin was atoned for and He could once again have a relationship with us. That is the goodness of God. That is the forgiveness of God. But for some of us, it just seems too good to be true. We have to learn to *receive* it.

This brings to mind an incident that happened about 15 years ago with my wife, Debbie. We were getting ready for church one morning, and at that time we lived in a very small house, with a very small bathroom. Any time we were getting ready to go somewhere, we had to do a bit of strategic maneuvering around each other in that tiny space. Anyway, Debbie was standing at the bathroom sink doing her face. She was still barefoot and in her bathrobe; but I was already dressed, complete with hard-sole dress shoes for church. I went into the bathroom to brush my teeth, and as I reached for something, the full weight of my entire body came down on her little toe!

She screamed—and at first her screams had no sound to them. She was in too much pain to make any real noise!

"I'm sorry, I'm sorry, I'm sorry!" I exclaimed over and over.

"It's OK—it's OK," Debbie said, as she hobbled toward the bed to sit down.

"I'm sorry, I'm sorry, I'm sorry!" I frantically repeated.

"I know," she said. "I know. It's OK—it was an accident."

I said, "No, no! I'm sorry, I'm sorry, I'm sorry!"

I kept saying it over and over again, and I think it was making her agony worse. She was probably thinking, *Just leave me alone and go away, will you?* But she said to me, "Really, it's OK! I forgive you."

I said, "No, no. I feel so bad! I feel so bad!"

And she kept saying to me, "It's OK."

Finally I said to her, "No, it is not OK. I want you to hit me!"

"What?" she said. "I don't want to hit you!"

"You don't understand," I said. "I feel bad, and I will feel better if you just hit me!"

The problem was not that Debbie was not *giving* forgiveness. The problem was that I wasn't *receiving* forgiveness. I wanted somehow to even the score between us!

Unfortunately, there are a lot of Christians who have a "Hit me" mentality. They have not received the forgiveness God freely has provided for them—so they want God to "hit" them. They think that if God hits them, it will make them feel better about the wrong they have done! This is the essence and origin of doing penance.

> *Until you receive the forgiveness*
> *God has freely given, you won't be*
> *able to give it to others.*

John 1:12 sets us straight on this point: "But as many as *received* Him, to them He gave the right to become children of God, to those who believe in His name" (emphasis added).

I want to just say it again: God will never hit you—because He already hit Jesus. Jesus bore our sins, completely and totally. Jesus paid the price for every sin you have ever committed so that you would not have to pay the price of forgiveness. *But you are going to have to receive it.*

And if you have a problem *giving* forgiveness, you probably have a problem *receiving* forgiveness. You must forgive others in the same way God has forgiven you. But until you receive the forgiveness God has freely given, you won't be able to give it to others.

If you have a problem *receiving* God's forgiveness, it could be because you have a problem *believing* it.

Believe

Perhaps you have a hard time believing God could really forgive you completely, totally releasing you from the penalty of sin. After all, how could a God who is pure and just and holy be able to accept us, when we have fallen so far short of His perfection?

The Bible does tell us that God is holy and pure. It says He is so pure that He cannot even look upon evil. Habakkuk 1:13 says, "You are of purer eyes than to behold evil, and cannot look on wickedness." So God cannot even look at evil! He cannot look at wickedness and sin. That is how pure His eyes are. And yet every one of us has missed it. Every one of us has sinned and done things God could not even put His eyes upon.

Isaiah 53:6 says, "All we like sheep have gone astray; we have turned, every one, to his own way." All of us have gone astray. All of us have transgressed God's commands. And God is so pure that He cannot look at our transgressions.

But Psalm 103:12 tells us, "As far as the east is from the west, so far has He removed our transgressions from us." God cannot look at our transgressions—*so He removed them*! He removed them so far away that He cannot see them anymore!

Job 36:7 says, "He does not withdraw His eyes from the righteous." And 1 Peter 3:12 says, "For the eyes of the LORD are on the righteous, and His ears are open to their prayers; but the face of the LORD is against those who do evil."

God is so pure that His eyes cannot even look on sin—but His eyes are on the righteous every day. You might be thinking, *I sure wish I was righteous. I sure wish God's eyes were upon me every day.*

This what you must believe: You *are* righteous! His eyes *are* upon you!

Second Corinthians 5:21 tells us: "For He made Him who knew no sin to be sin for us, that we might become the righteousness of God in Him." God made Jesus, who knew no sin, to be *made sin* for us—who were filled with sin. And He did that so that we could be *made righteous*, just as He is righteous. So *we* could be made the *righteousness of God Himself!* And all of this is done "in Him"—in Christ Jesus! When we receive the forgiveness Jesus paid for on the Cross, we are *made righteous.* We are made the righteousness of God!

It is true that God cannot look on sin. God had to do something about our sin just so He could look at us. And God did do something with our sin. He laid all of our sin on the Lord Jesus Christ. Through Jesus Christ, He has removed our transgression from us, as far as the east is from the west (see Ps. 103:12). All of my sin has been laid on Jesus, and all of my sin has been removed from me. Now God can look at me. Now He can talk with me, and He can walk with me all day long.

Because of what Jesus did, I can have a relationship with God. It is not because I did something good, and not because I somehow earned it. The reason I can have a relationship with God is because God laid all of my iniquity on His Son Jesus Christ. Because of what Jesus did for me, I can stand before God without guilt or sin or shame.

I am perfect now in the eyes of God. When He looks at me, He sees me washed in the blood of Jesus—and that blood makes me pure and holy in His sight. So God is looking upon me. His eyes are upon me every day, because He has made me righteous in His sight—not because I do righteous things. The only way He could make me righteous in His sight was through the blood atonement of His Son Jesus Christ.

I am telling you that *God has removed your sin!* You can have a relationship with Him now. Every day He wants to walk with you. He wants to talk with you.

Why am I telling you this? Because I want you to understand that you are forgiven! You have been completely pardoned by the sacrifice of Jesus Christ! And *because you have been pardoned, you can now pardon others.* Because you've been forgiven, you can now forgive!

It doesn't matter what anyone else has done to you. Is it worse than all the wrong you've ever done in your whole life? Think of all the wrong you have ever done—God has forgiven all of it. You have been forgiven. Now you need to share that forgiveness!

I want to tell you a wonderful story of forgiveness. This is the true story of a young Jewish man named Yakov and a young Jewish girl named Rachel; they lived in Europe during the time of the Holocaust. Yakov was in his early 20s and Rachel was a teenager—but Rachel had already caught Yakov's eye. He was falling in love with her.

But times were terrible for the Jews—and getting worse by the day. One night, Rachel's parents gathered a group of young people around them and said, "We have come to believe that no one is going to make it out of here alive. We think the Nazis are planning to kill us all—so we want you to try to escape." Then they took all the money they had and sewed it into Rachel's coat. "Maybe this will help to keep you alive," they told her. "It will be of no use here."

So that night Rachel and her sister, along with Yakov and about 20 other young people, made an attempt to escape from the Nazis. In the escape attempt Rachel's sister was shot, and Rachel ran back to help her. But it was no use—Rachel's sister died in her arms. Then Rachel was shot in both legs, and it seemed she too was going to die. But two boys grabbed her by the arms and dragged her into the woods to safety.

What were they to do with Rachel? She needed medical care or she would die. They were desperate—so they took her to the house of a German family. "Please help her," they said. "Look, she has money, and you can have all of it if you will take care of her." So the German family took Rachel into their home. They treated her wounds and told everyone that she was one of their own children. So Rachel lived with that family, and in this way she survived the war.

Things were more difficult for Yakov and the other young men. Yakov and about 15 other young men lived in the forest for over a year. They dug a large pit in the ground and covered it up to conceal themselves. They would sneak into town at night and forage for food, then go back to the forest and hide during the day.

After about a year someone found out about their hiding place. Soon Nazi soldiers came to the pit in which they were hiding. The young men were apprehended and sent to a prison camp.

When they arrived at the prison camp, the German commandant came out of his office and looked at his young prisoners.

"Are any of you boys a tailor?" he asked.

"I am a tailor, sir," said Yakov.

"You step over here, then," the commandant ordered. And then he had the other young men stand in a line.

Immediately Yakov realized they were going to shoot all of his friends. So he shouted out, "I must have an assistant! I can't sew clothes without an assistant!"

"All right," the commandant said. "Then I will let you pick one—only one though. You choose one of them."

Yakov had lived with all of those young men for over a year, as they struggled to survive in the forest. Among them were two brothers who were Yakov's best friends. In a split second, Yakov had to choose which one lived and which one died. So he chose one of the two brothers. The boy came over to where Yakov was standing—and then the Nazis shot the rest of the boys, as Yakov and his friend watched.

Yakov's ability to sew had saved his life—and he made it through the rest of the war by sewing uniforms for the German soldiers at the camp. Toward the end of the war, the Russian army was getting closer and closer to the camp, and the Nazi guards were afraid of being captured by the Russians. They made plans to escape on horses, and so they gave orders to Yakov and his friend to go and get their horses saddled for them. But as soon as those horses were saddled, the boys jumped on the horses and rode as fast as they could toward the Russian lines. Yakov and his friend safely escaped and ended up surviving the war.

Soon the years of unspeakable horror had passed, but Yakov had not forgotten about Rachel. He went looking for her after the war; and after he found her, they were married—and became Mr. and Mrs. Yakov Walden. They had a son and named him Marty, and he later became a rabbi. When Marty was growing up, it used to bother him that he didn't have any relatives. People would ask, "Are you related to these Waldens or those Waldens?" Marty dreaded that question—because he always had to say, "No, I'm not related to anyone." All of his grandparents, uncles and aunts had been killed in the Holocaust. Only one sister of his parents had survived.

It is my privilege to know Rabbi Marty Walden as a friend. I pastor a church in Dallas, Texas, and Rabbi Walden also pastors a church in that area. Rabbi Walden leads one of the largest congregations of Messianic Jews in the world.

Several years ago, Marty went to the death camp at Auschwitz to see where his grandparents had died. And the man who accompanied him on the trip was the grandson of a Nazi prison guard. These two men stood in Auschwitz—the grandson of a Jewish Holocaust victim and the grandson of a Nazi prison guard—and they hugged there and they prayed. Together they asked God to forgive the sins that had taken place there.

How could that happen? How could those two men do that? Only through the forgiveness God extends. The only way these two men were able to do that is because they had first received God's forgiveness—so they could give His forgiveness freely to others.

Like Marty and his friend, God has sorrow because of our sins—but He does not hold them against us. Through Jesus, He has provided forgiveness for every sin that we have ever—or will ever—commit. And when we receive His forgiveness, we are able to give it to others. We are able to forgive others as He has forgiven us.

Perhaps you are hurting—hurting over things that have happened to you, things that were unjust. Why allow that hurt to live on? God has made a way through Jesus for every wrong to be forgiven. He has already paid the price for every sin. And now, in His grace, He is asking, "Will you forgive the same way that I have forgiven you? Will you release that person fully and freely, and let it go?"

When you hold on to unforgiveness, you are the one being hurt. But when you forgive, you will be gloriously free. Free of torment, free of judgment—and free to move forward into the destiny that God has planned for your life.

CHAPTER TEN

THE PURPOSE TEST

Twenty-two years had passed since Joseph was sold into Egypt. He had spent 13 years working as a slave—and part of that time had been served in a dungeon, punished for a crime that he did not commit. Now, at 39 years of age, Joseph had already been the administrator of Egypt for 9 years. He had seen that country through the years of plenty, and now he was helping the country thrive during the early years of the famine. And Joseph was about to receive a surprise.

Suddenly, after more than two decades, the brothers who had betrayed him and caused him so much suffering were right before his eyes. And they were *bowing down before him*, with their faces to the earth (see Gen. 42:6)—just as his dreams had depicted symbolically so many years before! The Bible tells us what Joseph was thinking in that moment: "Then Joseph remembered the dreams which he had dreamed about them" (Gen. 42:9).

In other words, Joseph had a sudden realization. He realized that what God had shown him in those dreams so many years before had been a part of His plan all along. Joseph finally understood the *purpose* that lay behind those dreams. What could have been a moment of supreme triumph, grief or even revenge, instead became a moment of revelation.

> Then Joseph said to his brothers, "I am Joseph; does my father still live?" But his brothers could not answer him, for they were dismayed in his presence. And Joseph said to his brothers, "Please come near to me." So they came near. Then he said: "I am Joseph your brother, whom you sold into Egypt. But now, do not therefore be grieved or angry with yourselves because you sold me here; for God sent me before you to preserve life. For these two years the famine has been in the land, and there are still five years in which there will be neither plowing nor harvesting. And God sent me before you to preserve a posterity for you in the earth, and to save your lives by a great deliverance. So now it was not you who sent me here, but God; and He has made me a father to Pharaoh, and lord of all his house, and a ruler throughout all the land of Egypt" (Gen. 45:3-8).

The Purpose Test: Understanding Your Destiny

When you read these verses, you can see that Joseph finally understood what his purpose was. He understood not only the dreams God had given him but also the *purpose* those dreams had foreshadowed. In understanding that purpose, Joseph realized that he had stepped into the destiny for which God had created him.

Joseph, in essence, was telling his brothers, "You don't seem to understand. It was God who sent me here. So I don't want you to be angry with yourselves. I don't want you to be upset or grieved or sad. I want you to forgive yourselves just as I have forgiven you. God had a *purpose* for my life. And it was in order to fulfill *His purpose* that He sent me here to Egypt!"

Joseph had been through many difficult experiences during those years—but he finally understood the purpose for everything he had gone through. At last he was able to clearly see the vision, the purpose and the destiny God had planned for his life.

Joseph had passed the Purpose Test.

Every one of us will take this test—because every one of us has a God-ordained purpose. Will you discover what your purpose is and step into the destiny God has for you? That is the Purpose Test.

Is it possible to understand your purpose and live it to the fullest? Absolutely—Joseph did! There are four keys that can help you to discover and fulfill the purpose that God has for you.

Believe That You Have a Purpose

It is the first of the famous Four Spiritual Laws—"God loves you and has a wonderful plan for your life."

In order to discover the purpose that God has for your life, you must first *believe* that you have one! God created you for a unique purpose. And you simply must *accept* that by faith. We know that God has an eternal purpose for everything; and we know that the Body of Christ has an overall purpose in God's eternal plan. But it is important to know that you, as an individual, have a *specific purpose* as well. God has a unique destiny for you—and you are the only one who can fulfill it.

God is a *"purpose-full"* God. He is not a "purpose-less" God! He didn't create anything without a purpose. Every animal, every plant, every tree, every person—including you!—every single one of God's creations has been created for a purpose. You must believe that! The Bible says God formed you in your mother's womb—and when He formed you, He had a purpose in mind. The psalmist says of God:

For You formed my inward parts; You covered me in my mother's womb. My frame was not hidden from You, when I was made in secret, and skillfully wrought . . . . Your eyes saw my substance, being yet unformed. And in Your book they all were written, the days fashioned for me, when as yet there were none of them (Ps. 139:13,15-16).

This verse tells us that God's purpose for you had been written in His book before you were even born! Yes, before God created you, He had a plan and purpose for your life. He wants you to discover what that purpose is. And He wants you to fulfill it to its wonderful fullest.

Do you realize that you have the intellect, ability, talent and gifting to do something special for God? He designed you for a special role—and you will never be truly happy until you discover what that role is. But when you discover your purpose and begin fulfilling it, your life will take on new energy and excitement.

An example that comes to mind from my own life involves the gift of preaching. I have a purpose for my life, and part of that purpose involves preaching. So preaching is a gift that I have—and I like to preach! I get pumped up when I preach. I am more energized when I preach that I am when I do anything else!

Years ago when I worked in the nursery at the church my wife and I attended, I discovered just what a difference a sense of purpose can make. Our children were small at that time, and parents with children in the nursery were required to work in the nursery once a month. Now I might be gifted to preach—but I am definitely *not* gifted to work in the nursery! Every time I worked in the nursery, I had to have a nap when I got home. Working in the nursery didn't energize me at all. On the contrary, I was totally and completely worn out by it! I remember dreading it every time my week to work in the nursery was coming around.

Oh, no, I would think to myself. *In two more weeks it will be my week to work in the nursery again.* Then I prayed, "Oh, God, would You please help me to get through this somehow?"

The Lord finally said to me, "What are you gifted to do?"

"I'm gifted to preach!" I said.

"Then preach!" the Lord replied.

So I decided to take the Lord's advice. The next week I went into that nursery ready to preach! I said to those little babies, "Open your Bibles to Isaiah. I'm going to share with you some truths from God's Word." Then I preached to those little babies. They just took it all in, as babies do—but when I left the nursery that day, I was jazzed! Instead of being worn out, I was energized.

Here is my point: When God created you, He had a specific purpose in mind. And He has given you a specific gifting related to that purpose. You need to find out what that gifting is—because when you discover the gifting God created in you, it will bring energy and excitement to your life. And as you begin to move in that gifting, you will begin to understand your purpose.

If you're not sure what your purpose is, just look at the way you have been created. If you look at the way something is made, it helps you to understand the purpose of that thing. Even examining the design of inanimate objects will give you clues to their purpose.

Let me use an extremely mundane example—a toilet plunger. If you had never seen a toilet plunger before, you could initially imagine all sorts of purposes for it. You might speculate that it could be used as a ring-toss game, a birdbath for hummingbirds—or maybe even a bizarre hat for bald people. But none of those ideas really makes much sense. When you look carefully at the way a plunger is made, it soon becomes obvious that it was created with a very specific purpose in mind. (I won't elaborate further.)

In the same way, God created you with a very specific purpose in mind. You have a very unique design—and "in the spirit" you are actually shaped like something! If you could see what you are shaped like "in the spirit," it would help you to understand your purpose. For example, if you were designed to have the ministry of deliverance, "in the spirit" you probably look a lot like that plunger I was just describing. (That gives you an idea of what I think of demons, doesn't it?)

Seriously though, God has a unique purpose for your life—and it is vitally important for you to believe that. *Believe* that He created you with a specific purpose in mind, and discover what that purpose is. As you move toward discovering His purpose for your life, you will also be moving toward your destiny.

Understand That God Is in Control

God is in control. If you truly believe this, it will serve as an anchor for understanding your purpose. And if you don't believe that God is in control, you will live in a very sad and bewildering world—a world without much purpose.

If you don't believe that God is in control, you will probably become a pessimist sooner or later, because you will see no solution to some of the bad things that happen. When you can't see the hand of God working, you will eventually reach a point where you see only the bad in everything. And that can cause you to lose sight of your purpose.

Because God is good, you can rest in the knowledge that He is working for good in every situation, no matter

(If you don't know whether you are an optimist or a pessimist, just ask your spouse or your best friend. He or she will know!)

But when you understand that God is in control, you begin to see the good in everything—because God is good! You know that God has a purpose; and you can rest in the knowledge that He is working for good in every situation, no matter what the circumstances are.

Joseph had this attitude about the things that had happened in his life. His brothers were dismayed in his presence because of all the evil they had done to him (see Gen. 45:3). But Joseph was not dismayed at all.

Joseph explained it to his brothers this way: "But now, do not therefore be grieved or angry with yourselves because you sold me here; for God sent me before you to preserve life" (Gen. 45:5).

Joseph understood that God was ultimately in charge. That's why he was able to believe that God was working, even in circumstances that were terribly wrong and unjust. Although his brothers' actions had caused him to suffer, Joseph believed that God was still in control. And because he believed that, Joseph could see the hand of God in his situation. He was able to see that God had a purpose for sending him to Egypt and that his Lord had been working out His purpose all along.

Joseph told his brothers:

And God sent me before you to preserve a posterity for you in the earth, and to save your lives by a great deliverance. So now it was not you who sent me here, but God; and He has made me a father to Pharaoh, and lord of all his house, and a ruler throughout all the land of Egypt (Gen. 45:7-8).

Joseph knew that his brothers had sold him into Egypt through spite and jealousy. He knew what they had done was wrong. But that did not stop Joseph from believing that God was still in control. In the midst of all his trials, Joseph believed that God was working out His purposes and His plans. We, too, must come to trust God as Joseph did. We must understand that God can take even the wrongs that are done to us and use them for our good.

God can do much more than that. God can also take our own mistakes and failures and turn them for our good. (As you know, we're often our own worst enemy.) I want you to know something very important: God is bigger than your mistakes and failures! And He's much bigger than your own thinking and reasoning.

God says: "For as the heavens are higher than the earth, so are My ways higher than your ways, and My thoughts than your thoughts" (Isa. 55:9). Our thoughts are not as high as God's thoughts. Because we are human, we sometimes overlook this truth. But we don't need to grieve over mistakes that we have made, as though our failures and shortcomings had the power to short-circuit the purposes of God.

Recently my son had an opportunity to embrace God's providence—and to decide not to grieve over what he viewed as a failure on his part. When he moved to Amarillo, we went with him to help him find an apartment and get settled. We didn't know that area, so we just did the best we could in finding an apartment to rent. But after he'd lived there for a while and had gotten to know that area better, he found some better places to live—for less money. We were talking about that recently when he came home for a visit.

He said, "I wish that I hadn't signed a 12-month lease. I wish that I had only signed a 6-month lease. Then I could move into a better place right now, and it would cost less."

"Did you pray about it when you rented the place you are in?" I asked him.

"Yes, I did," he replied.

"OK," I said. "Then don't grieve over that decision. If you prayed about it and made the best decision you could at that time, then you need to trust in God. You need to understand that God has a way that He can eventually turn that decision for your good. Who knows? In six months you might find an even better place to live, for even less money. You don't know what God has planned! Or you could even be living in another city by that time. We don't know everything that the future holds."

In less than a week after that conversation, he went to the apartment office to check on getting out of his lease. He learned that even though he thought he had signed a 12-month lease, he had actually signed a 6-month lease and still received the benefits of a 12-month lease, which was one whole month's rent free. He was able to move into the better place for less money, and he learned the valuable lesson that God is in control even when we think that we've messed up and there is no way out!

When you have made a decision and you are not sure whether it was the right one or the best one, don't get upset second-guessing yourself about it. Don't say, "Oh, that was probably a terrible decision. I shouldn't have done that"—as though one mistake will derail you from your destiny. Instead, trust that God is in control. Say, "God, I believe that You are working out Your purposes in my life. You can take this decision and turn it for my good. I know that You are in control, so please show me what You are doing in this situation."

God is absolutely and totally in control. You must believe that—because if God is not in control, you need to find out who is and pray to him instead! Some Christians act as though they believe that the devil is in control instead of God—and he is not!

I don't know if you know this, but God and the devil are not in a fight with each other. We might be in a fight with the devil—but God is certainly not! God has already won the fight and defeated the devil. If you think God and the devil are anywhere close to being equal, I feel sorry for you, because they are not comparable in any way!

Satan has no power compared to God's awesome might. God has all the power in the world (and out of the world). If we are serving God, we do not need to be afraid of Satan—because God is the One who has the power! We serve the God of all power, and He is in control of our lives—so even when we make a mistake, God can turn it so that it ultimately works for our good. When we truly understand that, we won't grieve over mistakes we have made.

Romans 8:28 tells us: "And we know that all things work together for good to those who love God, to those who are the called according to His purpose." This verse tells us that God is working all things together for our good. It also says that God has called us "according to His purpose." God has a purpose! He has a divine purpose and an eternal plan, and each one of us is called to be a part of that purpose collectively. Within that eternal plan, He is working everything for our good!

But God also has a *specific* purpose and plan for each one of us individually. God has a *specific* purpose for you—and it is a part of His larger plan and His larger purpose. He is working in your life to bring about His plans and purposes. He is working in every situation you might face. And He can turn even bad decisions into good works for you when you are walking with Him—because He is in control.

Isaiah explains this mystery of God's providence:

For as the rain comes down, and the snow from heaven, and do not return there, but water the earth, and make it bring forth and bud, that it may give seed to the sower and bread to the eater, So shall My word be that goes forth from My mouth; it shall not return to Me void, but it shall accomplish what I please, and it shall prosper in the thing for which I sent it (Isa. 55:10-11).

Do you fully understand what God is saying to us in this Scripture passage? God is saying that every time He speaks, His Words will achieve His purpose. Every time! There will never be an occasion when God speaks and His Words do not produce results. He says that His Words will never come back to Him empty—His Words will always achieve the purpose for which He sent them. That is amazing! When God speaks, His purposes are going to come to pass!

Why is this so exciting? Because *God has spoken over you!* God spoke His purpose over your life when He created you! And the words God has spoken over your life will not return to Him void. They will accomplish the thing that He sent them to do.

So trust Him. Trust that He is working for your good in every situation. Trust that He has spoken over your life—and that His Word will accomplish what He purposed for your destiny.

Discover Your Gift and Your Direction

An important key to understanding your purpose can be found in discovering the gifts God has given you. Remember, God has designed you with a purpose in mind. So the gifts He has given you will always be related to your purpose in some significant way. If you just look at the gifts God has given you, they will tell you a lot about your purpose. Those gifts can help you understand your destiny in God.

If you're not sure what your purpose is, ask yourself these questions: What has God gifted me to do? What am I good at doing? What jazzes me? What gets me excited? What floats my boat? What churns my butter? When something energizes you and causes you to get excited, it is probably related in some way to your gift and to your purpose.

All too often we have wrong thinking about the plans God has for us and about the reasons God made us the way we are. Our thoughts might go something like this: *Well, this particular thing is what truly excites me. This is what I would really like to do with my life. But I suppose that isn't God's will for me. I suppose God probably wants me to do something dull or unpleasant.*

I don't know where we got that sort of thinking. Why would a good and loving God call you to do something that you don't even like to do?

I have to admit that I had ideas like that about God when I was growing up. I can remember thinking that if I wanted to serve God, I would probably have to marry an ugly woman and move to Africa. How ridiculous! Now, please don't misunderstand me—if you like moving to Africa and you like being married to an ugly woman, then you may be called to do that. But only if that is what you like!

When we are using the gifts God has given us, our lives are more exciting and fulfilling.

Our God is a good God! He wants you to have fun serving Him! He wants you to enjoy life as you serve Him!

Does the Bible say, "For God so loved the world that He gave His only begotten Son—*so that He can ruin our lives*"? No, that is not what the Bible says! Jesus said, "I have come that they may have life, and they may have it more abundantly" (John 10:10). Jesus came to give us life, and life that is *more abundant*. A more abundant life is a life filled with more good things, not less!

God wants to give us good things. He wants us to enjoy the life He has given us. So He has designed us with gifts and desires that are suited to His purpose for us. When we are using the gifts God has given us, our lives are more exciting and more fulfilling.

When you do the things that God has purposed for your life, you will be happy and fulfilled. So you need to discover your gifting! And remember that the gift that God has given you will be something that you like to do.

While there are probably as many unique giftings as there are people that God has created, the Bible describes seven specific gifts and encourages us to use those gifts "according to the grace that is given to us" (Rom. 12:6). In other words, these gifts come to us by the grace of God. So it is important for us to understand our gifting and use it according to God's design. Paul talks about this in Romans.

> For as we have many members in one body, but all the members do not have the same function, so we, being many, are one body in Christ, and individually members of one another. Having then gifts differing according to the grace that is given to us, let us use them: if prophecy, let us prophesy in proportion to our faith; or ministry, let us use it in our ministering; he who teaches, in teaching; he who exhorts, in exhortation; he who gives, with liberality; he who leads, with diligence; he who shows mercy, with cheerfulness (Rom. 12:4-8).

Paul says that just as our physical body has different parts with different functions, each of us has a different function in the Body of Christ. None of the parts of the physical body has the same purpose; but each part has a specific purpose that is an important part of the whole. In the same way, we as individuals each have a specific purpose that is an essential part of the Body of Christ. If we don't find that purpose and do it, the Body of Christ will be missing an important part!

Paul mentions seven specific giftings, which are often described as motivational gifts—in other words, gifts that spring out of the deep motivations in our nature. What follows here is just a brief overview of these seven gifts. I have given titles to these gifts that may help us to understand them and remember them.

Motivator ("Prophecy" [v. 6]). A person with the gift of prophecy desires to motivate other people to serve God. He or she desires to reveal the motive of people and see conformity to God's will. They tend to focus on "right" and "wrong." Those who have this gift are very interested in the motives within people's hearts. (Unfortunately, when a person with this gift is immature, he or she may be too judgmental about the motives of others.)

Servant ("Ministry" [v. 7]). The Greek word for "ministry" in this verse actually means "attendance" as a servant or "service."[1] A person with this motivational gift desires to meet the needs of people on a practical basis. When you go out to eat at a restaurant, a person with this gift will start to clean the table off after you have finished eating. Although the waiter might be standing right there, a person with a "servant" gift just can't resist pulling the dishes together and wiping the crumbs off the table. People with the gift of serving will be motivated to serve others wherever they may go.

Teacher (v. 7). The teacher is a person who loves to study and to present truths to people. These are people who like to read more than one book at once. They also write me e-mails with questions such as this: "Pastor Robert, I know that you're busy—but could you please just answer one question for me? *Could you please explain the book of Revelation?*" People with a teaching gift just can't seem to get enough of studying God's Word! (By the way, I don't want to get any more of those e-mails, all right? You see, I can't explain the book of Revelation to you— I'm still trying to understand it myself!)

Encourager (or "Exhorter" [v. 8]). Those with the gift of exhortation just love to exhort people and encourage people. We all know people with this gift. No matter what you say, they will try to encourage you. If you say, "I just lost my job," an exhorter will say, "Don't worry about it. You'll get a better job." If you say, "My house just burned down," an exhorter will say, "Well, it was old anyway. God will give you a better house."

Giver (v. 8). A giver is a person who desires to meet the material needs of others. Those who have this motivational gift absolutely love to give.

They are thrilled when they have the opportunity to meet a financial need.

Administrator (or "Leader" [v. 8]). A leader is a person who desires to help people through the gift of organization and administration. This is a person who has his or her socks organized by color and by style—and if you get a sock out of order, watch out! I have a man on my staff named Ed who has the gift of administration. I hired him for that purpose. His gift is very evident when he comes into my office and happens to notice that something is one inch out of place. His organizational gift will immediately manifest, and he can't help but move that item back by one inch to its "proper" location. (Of course, after he leaves my office I move it back again—just to annoy him!)

Sympathizer (or "Mercy" [v. 8]). The person who has this gift desires to identify with people and to empathize with them. My wife has this gift. (Interestingly enough, she has the gift of mercy, and I have the gift of prophecy—two gifts that many consider to be opposite of one another. But it is a good thing, because God balances each of us through the gift that is in the other!)

Each of these gifts is different, and each of these gifts has a part to play in fulfilling the purposes of God. If you've ever served on a team, you've probably had an opportunity to witness these gifts in action. For example, if you had a committee meeting, the meeting would probably be led by the "administrator"—who would start by passing out an outline, with detailed notes organizing the structure of the meeting. But if someone should mention in passing that Brother So-and-So has just lost his job, you would suddenly see all of the different motivational gifts going into action.

The prophecy-gifted person might say something like this: "He probably has sin in his life. Maybe we should go and confront him about that, and help him get the sin out of his life."

The teacher would say, "If he would just do what it says in 1 Timothy 3, he would be just fine. There are seven principles in 1 Timothy 3 that give the answer to this problem (they all begin with the same letter, by the way)—and he needs to know what those principles are."

The encourager would already be on the phone, calling the person who lost his job. The encourager would say something like this: "I heard that you lost your job, but it will be all right. God will get you a better job, and you'll be happier."

The person with the serving gift would have left the meeting by that time—to go and mow the person's yard for him.

The giver would probably be trying to take up an offering for the man who had lost his job. He would be saying, "OK, how much do you think he needs? We could take an offering right here in this room today and help this guy out."

And the mercy-motivated person? Why, the mercy-motivated person would be sitting over in the corner, crying tears of compassion for that man and his family—and would already be thinking about picking up a card for him on the way home and mailing it!

That is just a light-hearted illustration of the different ways that these gifts work to meet the needs of people. Remember, God's heart is always about people—so every one of these gifts has to do with people! Whatever your purpose in life, it will be related to other people in one way or another.

Each of these gifts is different, and each one has a part to play. All of these gifts have to do with helping people! And each gift will be motivated to help in a different way.

Together all of these gifts make up the Body of Christ.

As a member of the Body of Christ, you have a gift, and your gift is an important part of God's plan. It is important for you to determine what your gift is and to begin moving in that gift. When you start to operate in your gift, it will give you a *direction*.

Your Purpose Gives Direction, Not Specifics

You may not have a specific picture of your final destination—but you do have a gift. And when you determine what your gift is, that will help to bring *direction* to your life. Once you determine your direction, you can begin moving in it. Your purpose provides *direction* toward your destiny, but it is important to understand that your purpose does not contain the *specifics* of your destiny.

Joseph had a dream from God, and it gave him vision and direction. But he didn't know what the final manifestation of that dream would look like. Joseph also had a gift from God, and that gift gave him purpose in his everyday life. But he didn't know the *specifics* of how that gift would be used in his destiny.

It is pretty obvious that Joseph had a gift of administration. While Joseph was a slave in Potiphar's house, he organized the house and became the overseer of the house (see Gen. 39:3-5). When Joseph was in the prison, he organized the prison, and became the overseer of the prison (see Gen. 39:21-23). We don't know much about the pit—but my guess is that it was the most organized pit ever!

It takes faith to keep moving in the direction of your purpose— especially when you don't know the specifics regarding what waits at the end of that journey!

Joseph seemed to understand that he had a gift of administration, and he was faithful to use that gift wherever he went. But Joseph didn't know the *specifics* of how that gift would play a part in his destiny. While he was serving as a slave in Potiphar's house and while he was organizing things in the prison, Joseph had no idea that he would one day be doing that for the entire nation of Egypt. God never showed Joseph the specific details about the destiny that He had planned.

It is important to understand this truth if you want to pass the Purpose Test—because your gift will only point you in the *direction* of your destiny. Your purpose will provide a *direction*, but it will not provide the *specifics*. This is where faith comes in. Because it takes faith to keep moving in the direction of your purpose—especially when you don't know the specifics of what waits at the end of that journey!

Are there specifics to your destiny?

Yes, there are.

Can you know the specifics of your destiny?

Yes, you can.

When can you know the specifics of the destiny God has for you?

After you have carried them out!

When you finally step into the destiny that God had in mind all along, you will understand the specifics of His plans for your life—but not before that!

As you move toward your destiny, you will have to keep walking by faith. You will not know the specifics. All you will really know for certain is that you have a gift and a direction from God. So you must *be faithful* to that gift. You must *be faithful* to the direction God has given you.

After you have stepped into your destiny, you will look back, just as Joseph did (see Gen. 45:5-8), and understand the specifics of your purpose. You will say, "Oh, now I understand why I had to go through that. Now I know why God brought me here. This is the reason God worked in my life in that way. This is the reason things happened the way they did. Now I understand the purpose of all those things that happened!"

When you finally step into your destiny, you will see the full picture of God's purpose—but not before. You can't see the picture before it happens. But you will be able to see the *direction*. This is a promise we have from God.

The Bible says, "Your word is a lamp to my feet and a light to my path" (Ps. 119:105). Notice that it doesn't say, "Your Word is a bright spotlight that allows me to see three miles down the road." No—it says God's Word is a lamp to your *feet*. That means that it shows you the *next step*. It shows you just enough light to take the next step in front of you. And that light is all that you need to keep moving toward your destiny.

You may not know what is at the end of that road in front of you. But if you are faithful and keep walking in the direction God has given you, He will guide you into His purpose for your life. He will lead you into the destiny that He has planned for you.

Your purpose is a *direction* toward your destiny, but it is not the specifics. So determine your direction and begin heading toward that. Then trust that God is in control. Allow Him to direct your steps into His purposes. Rest in the knowledge of His goodness.

Let me tell you a few things about a man who had a purpose and a gift. He was faithful to develop his gifts. He headed in the direction that his gifts brought him—but I am certain he had no idea of the *specific destiny* to which that purpose would lead him!

- In his twenties, he failed in business twice, was defeated for the legislature and had a nervous breakdown; even worse, the woman he deeply loved died before they could be married.
- In his thirties, he was defeated for Congress, was later elected to Congress and later was defeated for Congress again.
- In his forties, he was defeated for the Senate and for the office of Vice President.
- However, at 51, he was elected President of the United States. His name was Abraham Lincoln.[2]

God put Abraham Lincoln in the right place at the right time. He became one of the most pivotal presidents in our nation's history, leading our country through a civil war that seemed certain to tear the nation apart. More important, he righted one of the greatest injustices in which our country has ever been involved—the institution of slavery. As He had done with Joseph, God put Abraham Lincoln right where He wanted him, at the exact moment in history when He needed him.

Abraham Lincoln faced many obstacles. While he was dealing with those obstacles, he had no idea of the *specifics* that God had planned for him. But he developed the gifts that he had, and he allowed those gifts to give direction and purpose to his life. Because he stayed focused on the *direction* God had given him, he was able to be where he needed to be, at the time when he needed to be there.

His gift and his purpose was to be a leader. But his destiny was to change the world.

Set Your Course and Be Faithful

We can all learn a lesson from Abraham Lincoln's example. Determine what your gift is and allow that gift to give you direction. Then *set your course* in that direction and simply *be faithful*. Don't get sidetracked trying to figure out the specifics. You get into problems when you try to dictate the specifics to God.

"But, God, I'm supposed to be a pastor. But, God, I'm supposed to be in business. But, God, I'm supposed to be a teacher. But, God, I'm supposed to . . . I'm supposed to . . . I'm supposed to."

What makes you think that you can tell God what you're supposed to do? He is God! He created you! Don't you think that He already knows what you're supposed to do?

When we imagine the specifics of our lives and they don't happen the way that we think they should, we are going to be disappointed. We might choose the city we think we're supposed to live in, the job we think we should have or the ministry we want to operate in. Then, if an event doesn't unfold the way we had planned, we say, "God, You're not keeping up Your end of the deal."

But all the while God is saying to us, "One step at a time. I have it all under control, within My plan and purpose. Just keep your eyes on Me, and take one step at a time—and I will take care of the specifics."

When we try to get involved in the specifics of our destiny, that is when we become discouraged. So don't get set on specifics. Instead, set your course in the direction God has shown you. And be faithful to what God has called you to do. Because it is faithfulness that will carry you through to the destiny God has planned.

The Lord has created every one of us with a purpose—but it is up to us to determine what we will do with that purpose.

The Lord sets a direction in front of each one of us—but it is our *faithfulness* that determines how far we will go.

There are many tests you must go through on the way to your destiny, and all of these tests are important. Humility, character, stewardship, integrity, perseverance—all of these are important to fulfilling your destiny. But they can all be summed up in one word: faithfulness.

Faithfulness is the answer to all the tests that God will give you. If you will just remain faithful to the direction that God has revealed to you, you will ultimately fulfill the destiny that God has on your life.

Will you be faithful to what God has called you to do?

What follows is an excerpt from the diary of a man who set his course and was faithful. His name was John Wesley.

Sunday a.m., May 5, preached in St. Ann's, was asked not to come back anymore.

Sunday p.m., May 5, preached at St. John's, deacons said, "Get out and stay out."

Sunday a.m., May 12, preached at St. Jude's, can't go back there either.

Sunday p.m., May 12, preached at St. George's, kicked out again.

Sunday a.m., May 19, preached at St. somebody else's, deacons called special meeting and said I couldn't return.

Sunday p.m., May 19, preached on the street, kicked off the street.

Sunday a.m., May 26, preached in a meadow, chased out of meadow as a bull was turned loose during the services.

Sunday a.m., June 2, preached out at the edge of town, kicked off the highway.

Sunday p.m., June 2, afternoon service, preached in a pasture, 10,000 people came to hear.[3]

John Wesley knew what his purpose was. He didn't see the *specifics* of that purpose—but he had a gift for preaching and he developed that gift. He allowed that gift to provide direction to his life. Then he set his course and he remained faithful. And faithfulness carried him through to his destiny in God.

More than anything else, it was faithfulness that kept Joseph true on the path to God's purpose. And faithfulness must also be the foundation for our lives. We must be faithful to God through all of these tests. As we travel the road to destiny, faithfulness is the anchor that will hold us steady through every storm. And faithfulness will keep us true until we pass every test and step into the fulfillment of our destinies in God.

May you live your God-given dreams to the fullest!

STAY
THE COURSE

All of us have a dream from God. And all of us have a divinely ordained destiny.

Chances are, as you read this, you are currently living in one of two places. You may be living in the wilderness land somewhere between your dream and your destiny. Or you may have stepped into that destiny and have already begun fulfilling it, but haven't completed it yet. In either case, you still have some tests to take and pass.

You see, some of the tests we've examined in this book occurred in Joseph's life after the dream but before the destiny. Some of these tests occurred after he began his destiny; but in order to fulfill his destiny to the fullest, he had to continue passing them.

Where are you on this road? Do you desire to see your dream become your manifest destiny? If so, you need to remember that it takes strong character to support big destiny.

That's why it's so important to allow God to work in these areas of your life. Allow Him to develop patience, purity, perseverance and true prosperity in your life. Allow Him to remove the pride and the wrong motives for wanting power. Allow your gracious heavenly Father to give you the grace to pardon those who have wronged you. Allow Him to reveal to you the glorious purpose for which He created you.

Don't get discouraged. He gave you the dream, and He is preparing you for the destiny. May you continue to allow God to strengthen and deepen your character, and may your God-given dream become your God-fulfilled destiny!

ENDNOTES

Chapter Two
1. Josephus, *Antiquities of the Jews,* bk. xii, ch. 11, sec. 3, quoted in *Jamieson, Fausset, and Brown Commentary.* CD-ROM, Biblesoft, 2003.

Chapter Three
1. *Adam Clarke's Commentary.* CD-ROM, Biblesoft, 2003.
2. *Biblesoft's New Exhaustive Strong's Numbers and Concordance with Expanded Greek-Hebrew Dictionary.* CD-ROM, Biblesoft and International Bible Translators, 2003. Hebrew ref. no. 6743; Greek ref. no. 2137.

Chapter Four
1. *Biblesoft's New Exhaustive Strong's Numbers and Concordance with Expanded Greek-Hebrew Dictionary.* CD-ROM, Biblesoft and International Bible Translators, 2003. Greek ref. no. 5343.
2. Ibid., Greek ref. no. 264.

Chapter Five
1. *Biblesoft's New Exhaustive Strong's Numbers and Concordance with Expanded Greek-Hebrew Dictionary.* CD-ROM, Biblesoft and International Bible Translators, 2003. Greek ref. no. 2744.
2. Ibid., Greek ref. no. 2172.

Chapter Six
1. *Biblesoft's New Exhaustive Strong's Numbers and Concordance with Expanded Greek-Hebrew Dictionary.* CD-ROM, Biblesoft and International Bible Translators, 2003. Hebrew ref. no. 1697.
2. Ibid., Hebrew ref. no. 565.

Chapter Eight
1. The Barna Group, "Tithing Down 62% in the Past Year," *The Barna Update,* May 19, 2003. http://www.barna.org/FlexPage.aspx?Page=BarnaUpdate&BarnaUpdateID=139 (accessed November 9, 2004).

Chapter Nine
1. *Biblesoft's New Exhaustive Strong's Numbers and Concordance with Expanded Greek-Hebrew Dictionary.* CD-ROM, Biblesoft and International Bible Translators, 2003. Hebrew ref. no. 5375.

Chapter Ten

1. *Biblesoft's New Exhaustive Strong's Numbers and Concordance with Expanded Greek-Hebrew Dictionary*. CD-ROM, Biblesoft and International Bible Translators, 2003. Greek ref. no. 1248.

2. "Abraham Lincoln," *commonplacebook.com*, 2004. http://www.commonplacebook.com/inspire/lincoln.shtm (accessed November 17, 2004).

3. "A Page from Wesley's Diary," *Life Enhancements*, September 2, 1999. http://lifeenhancements.tripod.com/Misc24.html (accessed November 17, 2004).